Blind BC

Blind Intersection?
Policy and the Automobile Industry

CLIFFORD WINSTON and ASSOCIATES

THE BROOKINGS INSTITUTION
Washington, D.C.

HD
9710
.U52
W55
1987

Library of Congress Cataloging-in-Publication Data:
Winston, Clifford, 1952–
  Blind intersection?

  Includes index.
  1. Automobile industry and trade—Government
policy—United States. I. Brookings Institution.
II. Title.
HD9710.U52W55 1987   338.4'76292'0973   87-806
ISBN 0-8157-9466-5
ISBN 0-8157-9465-7 (pbk.)

987654321

THE BROOKINGS INSTITUTION is an independent organization devoted to nonpartisan research, education, and publication in economics, government, foreign policy, and the social sciences generally. Its principal purposes are to aid in the development of sound public policies and to promote public understanding of issues of national importance.

The Institution was founded on December 8, 1927, to merge the activities of the Institute for Government Research, founded in 1916, the Institute of Economics, founded in 1922, and the Robert Brookings Graduate School of Economics and Government, founded in 1924.

The Board of Trustees is responsible for the general administration of the Institution, while the immediate direction of the policies, program, and staff is vested in the President, assisted by an advisory committee of the officers and staff. The by-laws of the Institution state: "It is the function of the Trustees to make possible the conduct of scientific research, and publication, under the most favorable conditions, and to safeguard the independence of the research staff in the pursuit of their studies and in the publication of the results of such studies. It is not a part of their function to determine, control, or influence the conduct of particular investigations or the conclusions reached."

The President bears final responsibility for the decision to publish a manuscript as a Brookings book. In reaching his judgment on the competence, accuracy, and objectivity of each study, the President is advised by the director of the appropriate research program and weighs the views of a panel of expert outside readers who report to him in confidence on the quality of the work. Publication of a work signifies that it is deemed a competent treatment worthy of public consideration but does not imply endorsement of conclusions or recommendations.

The Institution maintains its position of neutrality on issues of public policy in order to safeguard the intellectual freedom of the staff. Hence interpretations or conclusions in Brookings publications should be understood to be solely those of the authors and should not be attributed to the Institution, to its trustees, officers, or other staff members, or to the organizations that support its research.

Foreword

IN THE PAST TWO DECADES the U.S. automobile industry has become a focus of national concern. The high value of the dollar against the yen and the accompanying flood of Japanese automobiles into the U.S. market caused severe financial losses and record layoffs in a U.S. industry that had once been the world leader. American automakers no longer seemed able to compete, and protectionist sentiment increased. Government was pressured to act quickly on this issue, and to deal with a wide range of industry-related issues such as ensuring the safety of automobile occupants.

In this book Clifford Winston and his associates evaluate government policies for increasing the competitiveness of U.S. automobile manufacturers and for solving social problems related to the automobile. These policies, the authors find, have had mixed success, and some, such as the voluntary export restrictions negotiated with the Japanese government, have exacerbated the very problems they were intended to alleviate. Thus policymakers genuinely concerned with their constituents' interests have often supported actions whose effects have turned out inimical to those concerns, effects that could have been anticipated if careful economic analyses had been performed.

Clifford Winston is a senior fellow in the Brookings Economic Studies program. His associates are Ana Aizcorbe, research economist at the Bureau of Labor Statistics; Ann Friedlaender, dean of humanities and social science, Massachusetts Institute of Technology; Fred Mannering, assistant professor of civil engineering, University of Washington; and Dennis Sheehan, assistant professor of management, Purdue University.

The authors wish to thank Katherine Abraham, James Berkovec, Menzie Chinn, Robert Crandall, Kenneth Flamm, Harry Katz, Robert Lawrence, Michael Levine, Mustafa Mohatarem and his associated staff, Steven Morrison, William Niskanen, and Alice Rivlin for reading the manuscript and making useful suggestions for improvement. They would especially like to thank Daniel McFadden and Kenneth Train for their insightful and constructive reviews of the manuscript.

Various individuals made important contributions to specific chapters. Chapter 2, which is partly based on Ana Aizcorbe's dissertation, received valuable comments from Ernst Berndt, Melvyn Fuss, and Richard Tresch; research assistance was provided by Joan Winston and Toshiki Yotsuzuka. Chapter 5 benefited from the comments of Ted Miller; research assistance was provided by Carolyn Gonot and Jamal Itani. Chapter 6 received valuable comments from John Chubb and Steven Smith; research assistance was provided by Karen Fuller.

James Schneider and Brenda Szittya edited the manuscript, Carol Evans and Almaz Zelleke verified its factual content, and David Rossetti processed it.

This study was funded by grants from the U.S. Department of Commerce and the Alfred P. Sloan Foundation.

The views expressed in this book are those of the authors and should not be ascribed to those persons or organizations whose assistance is acknowledged or to the trustees, officers, or other staff members of the Brookings Institution.

BRUCE K. MACLAURY
President

February 1987
Washington, D.C.

Contents

Figures

CHAPTER ONE

Introduction and Summary

CLIFFORD WINSTON

FROM THE END of World War II to the mid-1960s the United States was the world leader in automobile production. In the past twenty years, however, that position has steadily eroded so that now the U.S. share of world motor vehicle production is less than 25 percent (figure 1-1). By 1985, Japanese auto production alone exceeded that of the United States. Perhaps more significantly, U.S. imports of Japanese cars have increased more than tenfold since 1950 (figure 1-2). If such sales trends continue, the U.S. industry will eventually be dominated by the Japanese in its home market.

This erosion has been accompanied by dramatic swings in the profits of U.S. motor vehicle and equipment manufacturers (figure 1-3) and in industry employment (figure 1-4). By 1980, record industry financial losses and large layoffs generated pleas from both management and labor for protection against a flood of imports. That protection was achieved when the Japanese agreed to limit their auto exports. In combination with a concurrent economic recovery it led to the industry's current financial rebound.

Import protection has not been the only recent public policy to have an important influence on the industry's performance. Government regulations for automobile safety, fuel economy, and emissions imposed in the 1960s and 1970s have collectively increased the cost and reduced the reliability of American vehicles.[1] Some argue the regulations are justified because U.S. producers have failed to pursue effectively the social goals of increased automobile occupant safety and fuel conservation. Thus the blame for the relative decline of the industry has been

1. Robert W. Crandall and others, *Regulating the Automobile* (Brookings, 1986).

1

Figure 1-1. World Motor Vehicle Production, 1950–85

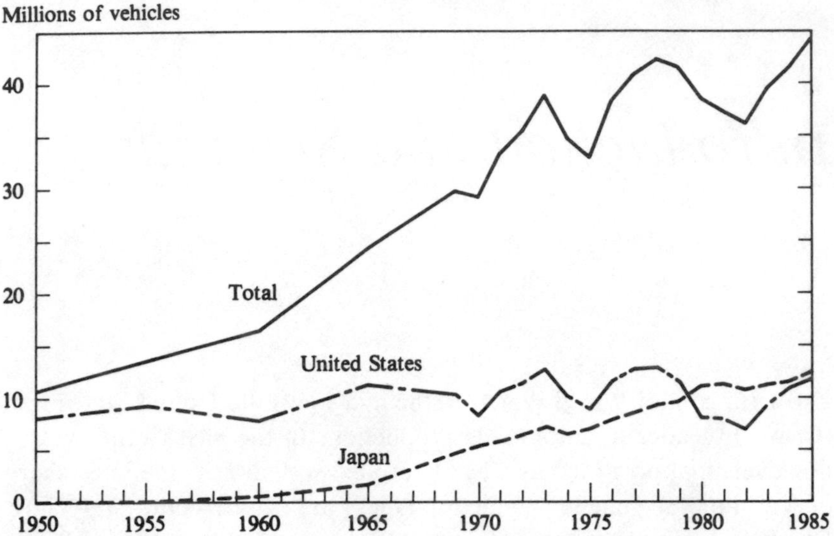

Millions of vehicles

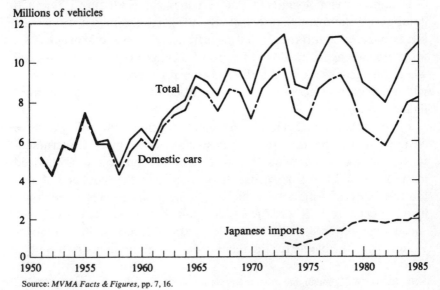

Source: Motor Vehicle Manufacturers Association of the United States, *MVMA Facts & Figures '86* (Detroit: MVMA, 1986), p. 28.

Figure 1-2. Retail Passenger Car Sales in the United States, 1951–85

Millions of vehicles

Source: *MVMA Facts & Figures*, pp. 7, 16.

Figure 1-3. U.S. Motor Vehicle and Equipment Manufacturers' Profits, 1973–85

Billions of dollars

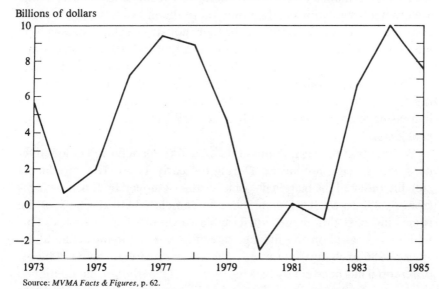

Source: *MVMA Facts & Figures*, p. 62.

Figure 1-4. U.S. Motor Vehicle and Equipment Manufacturing Average Employment, 1966–85

Production workers
(annual average, thousands)

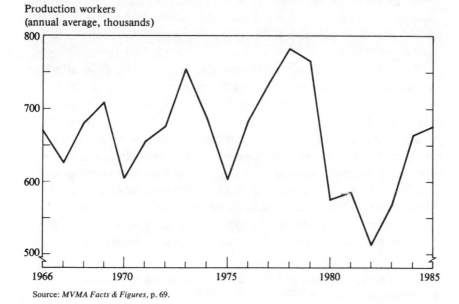

Source: *MVMA Facts & Figures*, p. 69.

placed on the industry itself, both management and labor. Others blame government regulations and inattention to the industry's needs. Whatever the source of the problem, further industry decline is viewed by many as causing such harm to the nation that industrial protection is justified. Others believe the industry can compete if it changes its ways.

The purpose of this book is to evaluate both the competitiveness of the U.S. auto industry and the effectiveness of government policy in increasing competitiveness and in solving automobile-related social problems.

We find that the U.S. automobile industry *can* achieve competitiveness with foreign producers. During the early 1980s, U.S. producers steadily reduced the marginal cost advantage enjoyed by Japanese firms from $2,300 to $1,300 for comparable vehicles, with the bulk of the remaining cost differential attributable to differences in wages. This finding was based on an exchange rate of 249.05 yen to the dollar; at the spring 1986 exchange rate of 167.50 yen to the dollar this $1,300 cost differential has been cut by two-thirds. Given that the yen has continued to appreciate against the dollar and U.S. producers are building more components of their vehicles overseas (outsourcing), thus taking advantage of low-cost foreign labor, the remaining cost differential is likely to be negligible. And U.S. industry sales for the remainder of the decade should be fairly strong, nearly 8 million vehicles annually, even without import restrictions. This level of sales should generate adequate profits for the industry, although industry employment may continue to fall because of outsourcing.

The U.S. government deserves mixed reviews for its policies affecting the industry.[2] By contributing to the fall in the value of the dollar during 1985–86, government economic policy has enhanced the competitiveness of the U.S. automobile industry. By not effectively supporting a program that provides trade adjustment assistance to autoworkers, however, the government has exacerbated tensions between management and labor over the industry's decision to use more overseas labor. Ironically, the greatest current threat to industry competitiveness is the voluntary export restrictions negotiated with the Japanese government. In response to the restrictions, Japanese firms have begun to locate production facilities in the United States. By producing automobiles and

2. One government initiative, the financial bailout of Chrysler Corporation in 1980, has clearly helped one member of the industry. This book does not, however, assess the social desirability of this policy.

trucks on American soil, they may significantly increase consumer preference for their vehicles. This unanticipated consequence should serve as a lesson to policymakers who believe that trade restrictions will benefit U.S. industries in the long run.

Given the increase in Japanese production capacity in America and the entry of new foreign producers, such as those from Yugoslavia and Korea, into the U.S. market, government policy can best help the U.S. automobile industry by contributing to an economic environment that does not present opportunities for established foreign firms to erode consumer preference for U.S. makes or provide new foreign entrants with opportunities to get a strong foothold in the U.S. market.

Government policies toward automobile-related social problems have not even fared as well as economic policies, and in some cases they have proved to be counterproductive and to have betrayed the intentions of the legislators who approved them. The voluntary export restrictions, which were supposed to increase employment in the U.S. auto industry, have actually reduced it, although industry wages remain high compared with those in the rest of the manufacturing sector. The major policy initiative to improve automobile occupant safety—laws mandating the use of seat belts—does not pass a cost-benefit test. Passive belts or airbags would appear to have greater net benefits. The 55 mph speed limit, however, has proved its worth and should be retained except perhaps on lightly traveled sections of rural interstates.

One important general conclusion is that automobile policies have too often been supported by policymakers who are genuinely concerned with their constituents' interests but who have not foreseen the actual effects of the policies. When such policies go awry, the social costs can be high. These effects could have been anticipated if careful economic analyses had been performed before legislation was initiated. In the future, economic analyses of these policies could not only be cost-effective but could prevent continued application of policies that are clearly misguided.

CHAPTER TWO

Cost Competitiveness of the U.S. Automobile Industry

ANA AIZCORBE, CLIFFORD WINSTON,
and ANN FRIEDLAENDER

SINCE the 1970s many observers have questioned the U.S. automobile industry's ability to compete effectively with foreign producers, particularly the Japanese, in an unrestricted market. Facts would suggest that America cannot compete. As chapter 1 showed, the share of the domestic automobile market belonging to foreign firms has increased more than tenfold since 1950. And the reason has partly been cost: U.S. automakers must spend an estimated $1,500 to $2,500 more than Japanese automakers to manufacture a comparable small car.[1] These costs are assigned various causes—inefficient management, deteriorating plants, more expensive materials—but they most often boil down to labor and productivity. American workers are allegedly paid too much to produce too little.

Industry defenders acknowledge the apparent truth of some of these claims. But they assign much of the blame to conditions the industry cannot control. The dollar-yen exchange rate, they say, has been so inflated that, even with all else being equal, a comparable Japanese car would still cost less than its U.S. counterpart. And, they add, all else is not equal. Among other things, capital costs too much.

This chapter assesses the cost competitiveness of the American automobile industry to determine whether changes in government economic policy and industry behavior could make the industry more

---

1. Estimates are surveyed in Michael S. Flynn, "Differentials in Vehicles' Landed Costs: Japanese Vehicles in the U.S. Marketplace," working paper series 3 (University of Michigan Joint U.S.-Japan Automotive Study, October 1982).

6

competitive. We estimate a cost function for the Big Three U.S. producers—General Motors, Ford, and Chrysler—and for the major Japanese producers, and calculate the difference in the U.S. and Japanese firms' marginal costs for producing vehicles of various sizes. We then analyze three potential sources of the cost differential: differences in prices of materials, labor, and capital; differences in technology; and differences in levels of productivity. Finally, we consider how changes in government economic policy and changes in behavior by U.S. manufacturers could achieve cost competitiveness.

Cost Functions and the Marginal Cost Differential

The analytical framework used here parallels the approach to estimating automobile cost functions taken by Friedlaender, Winston, and Wang.[2] We specify a multiproduct cost function and factor demand equations using the firm as the basic unit of observation. Total costs of domestic automobile operations are a function of factor prices (user cost of capital, price of labor, and composite price of materials); number of vehicles produced, by size classification; and a time variable.[3] The factor

2. Ann F. Friedlaender, Clifford Winston, and Kung Wang, "Costs, Technology, and Productivity in the U.S. Automobile Industry," *Bell Journal of Economics*, vol. 14 (Spring 1983), pp. 1–20. This paper provides rigorous justification for most of the procedures used here. In particular, our approach recognizes that the cost function must control for different degrees of vertical integration between U.S. and Japanese firms and that each firm's output (number of vehicles produced, by size classification) should be treated as endogenous. In addition, we assume that both U.S. and Japanese firms are able to adjust their capital stock in an optimal fashion on an annual basis, and thus we estimate a long-run cost function. This assumption is not unreasonable because substantial changes in investments and scrappage do occur on an annual basis, and new models can often be developed with minimal capital investment. Indeed, expenditures on special tooling by the automobile industry represent a very small fraction of total industry costs. For instance, Lee Iacocca states that Ford was able to develop the Mustang for a mere $75 million by taking advantage of existing components from the Falcon line. See Lee Iacocca with William Novak, *Iacocca: An Autobiography* (Bantam Books, 1984), p. 66. Similar examples could be produced for the other U.S. and Japanese manufacturers.

3. The multiproduct cost function can be written as $C = C(Y, W, T)$, where C represents total costs, Y_i is the physical level of output i, W is the vector of factor prices, and T is the time variable. Friedlaender, Winston, and Wang's cost specification (see "Costs, Technology, and Productivity") included hedonic attributes of the vehicles, for example, cylinder capacity, to control for vehicle quality and technological conditions. Such effects were generally found to be statistically insignificant in that study and in the empirical work carried out here. Thus our analysis disregards these effects.

demands, which are influenced by the same variables, are the number of domestic employees, units of capital (total capital costs divided by user cost of capital), and pounds of materials. We use a quadratic specification of the cost function, which yields linear factor demand equations.[4] The functional specification of the cost and factor demand equations, the estimation procedure, and estimates of the complete set of parameters are presented in appendix A to this chapter.

The data base used for this analysis is a pooled, cross-section time series sample of General Motors, Ford, and Chrysler for the period 1958–83 and of the major Japanese automobile manufacturers, Toyota, Honda, Nissan, Isuzu, Suzuki, Toyo-Kogyo (Mazda), Daihatsu, and Fuji, for the period 1970–82.[5] A detailed description of the data, the construction of the variables, and summary statistics are presented in appendix B to this chapter.

To facilitate a cost comparison, outputs were classified as motorcycles and minicars (produced only by the Japanese), and small cars, large cars, and trucks. The weight and wheelbase of the small cars were virtually the same for U.S. and Japanese firms. Because U.S. firms produce cars such as Cadillacs that are heavier and have a longer wheelbase than any produced by the Japanese, vehicle size in the large car classification is not comparable between U.S. and Japanese firms. This is also true for trucks.[6]

Estimates of the first-order coefficients for U.S. and Japanese qua-

---

4. The quadratic specification is particularly attractive to use in multiple-output cost functions because it permits an easy analysis of marginal costs and economies of scale and scope. It has, however, been criticized for its inability to impose the homogeneity condition needed for cost minimization. But the use of the translog approximation, which can impose this condition, presents problems here because small cars were not produced by some manufacturers in the early portion of our sample. It is possible to use a Box-Cox transformation in a translog specification to circumvent the problem of zero values, but this transformation may impose constraints on the properties of the cost function as it varies through output space that are difficult to evaluate. See William J. Baumol, John C. Panzar, and Robert D. Willig, *Contestable Markets and the Theory of Industry Structure* (Harcourt Brace Jovanovich, 1982), chap. 15.

5. The sample for the U.S. and Japanese producers is for domestic production. American Motors could not be included with the Big Three U.S. producers because of significant differences in technology related to its smaller scale of operations and lack of vertical integration. Extending the Japanese sample before 1970 created empirical problems because some manufacturers did not make any vehicles in some size classifications.

6. Because we did not control explicitly for vehicle quality (see note 3), quality differences may exist between comparable car classifications.

Table 2-1. First-Order Coefficients of U.S. and Japanese Cost Functions for Vehicle Production

Regressor	U.S. coefficient[a]	Japanese coefficient[a]	Interpretation
Constant	17,368,530 (335,373)	647,887,865 (7,455,717)	Total costs[b]
Motorcycle output	. . .	67.536 (9.697)	Marginal cost of a motorcycle[b]
Minicar output	. . .	278.874 (86.796)	Marginal cost of a minicar[b]
Small car output	3.414 (1.519)	554.171 (24.099)	Marginal cost of a small car[b]
Large car output	5.010 (0.394)	572.323 (324.533)	Marginal cost of a large car[b]
Truck output	9.395 (1.395)	2,242.696 (180.625)	Marginal cost of a truck[b]
Price of capital	113,271.5 (5524.0)	947,547.30 (57,267.20)	Index of capital demanded
Price of labor	279,656.8 (5119.4)	23,782.82 (601.728)	Number of workers demanded[c]
Price of materials	13,009,212 (159,824)	2,832,482 (22,138.1)	Pounds of materials demanded[d]
Time	90,236.44 (60,121.7)	526,593.50 (1,776,497)	Average change in total cost over time

Sources: Authors' calculations based on data described in appendix B to this chapter.

a. Asymptotic White heteroskedastic-consistent standard errors are in parentheses. See appendix B to this chapter for full regression results.

b. Total costs and marginal costs are in thousands of 1975 dollars for U.S. coefficients and thousands of 1975 yen for Japanese coefficients, all variables at their sample mean.

c. Wages per worker are in thousands of 1975 dollars for U.S. coefficients, thousands of 1975 yen for Japanese coefficients.

d. Materials price is in 1975 dollars or yen per pound of materials.

dratic cost functions are presented in table 2-1. Each coefficient can be interpreted as the effect of a given variable on total cost, holding all other variables at their sample mean. Factor prices and outputs have a positive, statistically significant effect on costs. The influence of time is statistically marginal, which implies very little growth in productivity for either country's auto industry. The estimates of costs are reasonable in that they indicate the marginal cost in 1975 dollars of producing a small car in the United States is $3,414, of a large car, $5,010, and of a truck, $9,395. The price–marginal cost markups for small cars and large cars are within the range of previous estimates.[7] The estimates of the marginal

7. We averaged manufacturers' list prices of small cars and large cars as defined by our classifications and obtained price–marginal cost markups for small cars and large cars of 12 percent and 6 percent respectively. Although the relative markups are inconsistent with conventional wisdom (in all likelihood because of the aggregation of

Table 2-2. Marginal Cost Differential of U.S. and Japanese Automakers for Small Cars, Selected Years, 1970–83

1975 dollars

Year	Manufacturing costs		Tariffs and transport costs (Japan only)	Differential
	United States	Japan		
1970	3,937	1,543	296	2,098
1975	4,391	1,972	296	2,123
1980	4,428	1,763	296	2,369
1981	3,505	1,800	296	1,409
1982	3,336	1,739	296	1,301
1983	3,333	n.a.	n.a.	n.a.
Sample mean	3,414	1,900	296	1,218

Source: Authors' calculations. Tariffs and transport costs in 1975 dollars are from the National Academy of Engineering, *The Competitive Status of the U.S. Auto Industry* (Washington, D.C.: National Academy Press, 1982). n.a. Not available.

costs for the Japanese industry indicate, as expected, that production costs increase with vehicle size.[8]

The empirical cost models are used to estimate the marginal cost differential between U.S. and Japanese automakers.[9] The results presented in table 2-2 include the manufacturing cost differential in 1975 dollars and tariffs and transportation costs borne by the Japanese.[10] As

---

the price data), the absolute markups are close to the price-cost margins of around 10 percent obtained by Timothy F. Bresnahan, "Departures from Marginal-Cost Pricing in the American Automobile Industry: Estimates for 1977–78," *Journal of Econometrics,* vol. 17 (November 1981), pp. 201–27.

8. The effect of vehicle size on cost for Japanese firms is relatively small because the difference in size between small and large Japanese cars is not nearly so great as the difference between small and large American cars. Data limitations prevent us from estimating a price–marginal cost markup for Japanese vehicles.

9. Based on our cost specification, estimates of the marginal cost of producing a given classification of vehicle are obtained by calculating

$$MC_i = \frac{\partial C}{\partial Y_i} = \alpha_i + \sum_m A_{im}(Y_m - \overline{Y}_m) + \sum_j E_{ij}(W_j - \overline{W}_j) + F_i(T - \overline{T}),$$

where the variables are as defined in note 3. Thus α_i represents the marginal cost of producing a given vehicle, all variables held at their sample mean. Marginal cost estimates at points other than the sample means are obtained by using the complete expression.

10. Results are presented in 1975 dollars because our estimated coefficients are in these units. The marginal cost differentials are based on the corresponding exchange rate (the rate at which goods were actually traded) for the year in question. In policy discussions later in this chapter, we evaluate the marginal cost differential at 1986 exchange rates, which reflect a significant appreciation of the yen.

our base case, we report marginal cost estimates at the sample means of the variables in our models.[11] The results indicate that the marginal cost of manufacturing and that of transporting (borne only by the Japanese) a small car to the United States is $1,218 greater for a U.S. firm than for a Japanese firm. Although this figure is within the range of previous estimates of the average differential based on accounting costs, it is an estimate of the marginal cost differential in a multiproduct framework and cannot be easily compared with the earlier findings.[12]

In the past few years, the marginal cost differential has declined significantly. Between 1970 and 1980 it was roughly $2,200; since 1980 it has declined to $1,300.[13] Despite the progress of U.S. automakers in reducing costs relative to the Japanese, however, a cost differential based on 1982 exchange rates still exists.

Sources of the Cost Differential

Conventional explanations for the cost differential tend to be based on alleged differences in the costs of funds and labor, and in productivity. We consider not only these elements but also differences in technology.

When we calculated a weighted average cost of funds for the U.S. and Japanese auto industries, using the methodology described in appendix B, we found only small differences (table 2-3).[14] The cost of funds was slightly lower for Japanese firms from 1965 to 1972, but has been higher in most years since then, and the mean for the entire period is almost identical for the industries. Hence, contrary to popular belief,

11. Although they are within the same classification, the mean sizes of U.S. and Japanese small cars are not likely to be identical. U.S. vehicles are usually heavier, thus causing the cost differential to be slightly overstated.

12. Previous estimates cited in Flynn, "Differentials in Vehicles' Landed Costs," refer to the average cost differential. Because average costs depend on product mix, they are not defined in a multiproduct cost setting.

13. The accuracy of our approximation for specific time periods is not so great as at the sample mean. With this in mind, one should reasonably consider this finding and others we report for specific time periods in terms of their qualitative significance.

14. We use the term cost of funds instead of the cost of capital because the latter typically refers to the user cost of capital, which includes items such as the purchase price of a unit of capital in addition to the cost of funds that are not necessary for our factor-price comparisons (see appendix B).

Table 2-3. U.S. and Japanese Automakers' After-Tax Weighted Average Cost of Funds, 1965–82ᵃ

Percent

Year	U.S. industry	Japanese industry
1965	14.2	9.6
1966	14.8	10.8
1967	16.8	9.3
1968	14.7	10.2
1969	16.6	11.4
1970	10.9	8.9
1971	8.3	8.3
1972	8.4	10.7
1973	10.0	12.1
1974	10.4	12.1
1975	6.3	10.3
1976	6.6	12.8
1977	6.8	9.9
1978	8.0	7.7
1979	9.1	8.2
1980	8.4	9.7
1981	9.1	10.9
1982	9.0	13.5
mean	10.5	10.4

Source: Authors' calculations based on sources in appendix B to this chapter.
a. Because we use the expected inflation rate, it is not accurate to say the figures in this table represent the real cost of funds. But they are closer to real than nominal values.

differences in the cost of funds are not a contributing factor to the cost differential.[15]

Differences in labor costs are significant, however. The mean compensation for all employees during 1982 was $19,175 (in 1975 dollars adjusted for 1982 exchange rates) for the American industry, $11,227 for the Japanese industry.

Differences in technology are reflected in different elasticities of

15. A widely cited study directed by George Hatsopoulos concludes that the cost of funds has been significantly higher in the United States than in Japan. This conclusion, however, is based on the assumption that the cost of funds in Japan is identical to the cost of debt, an inappropriate assumption because most Japanese automakers have as much outstanding equity as debt. The imprecisions caused by this assumption are avoided here because we use a weighted average of the cost of debt and equity. See George N. Hatsopoulos, "High Cost of Capital: Handicap of American Industry" (unpublished paper, American Business Conference, Washington, D.C., April 1983).

Table 2-4 U.S. and Japanese Automobile Industry Factor Demand Price and Cross-Price Elasticities Evaluated at Sample Means

	Labor		Capital		Materials	
Prices	United States	Japan	United States	Japan	United States	Japan
Labor	−0.3310	−0.2630	0.2241	0.3248	−0.0089	−0.0055
Capital	0.1877	0.2271	−1.1180	−0.6110	0.0916	0.0144
Materials	−0.0154	−0.0452	0.1880	0.1693	−0.0500	−0.0200

Source: Authors' calculations based on sources in appendix B to this chapter.

factor demand, multiproduct scale economies, and economies of scope.[16] Factor demand elasticities measure how firms' demands for labor, capital, and materials change in response to changes in the prices of these factors, while economies of scale and scope indicate whether the industry's level of production and mix of vehicle types are efficient. Calculating these measures can determine whether significant differences exist between the U.S. and Japanese automakers and, if they do, whether they contribute to the cost differential.

Estimates of the factor demand elasticities for U.S. and Japanese automakers in table 2-4 show that for automakers in both countries capital and labor and capital and materials are substitutes, while labor and materials are complements. The magnitudes of the elasticities and cross-elasticities are also similar in the two industries. The differential in production costs is therefore not attributable to differences in the industries' responsiveness to changes in the prices of labor, capital, or materials.

Table 2-5 presents estimates of multiproduct scale economies for U.S. and Japanese automakers from 1970 to 1983. An estimate greater than 1.0 implies economies of scale; an estimate less than 1.0, diseconomies of scale. An estimate of exactly 1.0 would imply constant returns to scale.[17] Large economies or diseconomies suggest inefficiencies. Large

16. Multiproduct economies of scale indicate the behavior of costs as the production levels of the firms' products change proportionately. Economies of scope indicate whether the total cost of producing a range of products jointly is less than the cost of producing each one separately. The theoretical development of the concepts of multiproduct scale economies and economies of scope can be found in Baumol, Panzar, and Willig, *Contestable Markets*.

17. Multiproduct scale economies, S_m, at a given point of production are defined by $S_m = C(Y)/\Sigma_i Y_i MC_i$. This expression can be interpreted as the ratio of costs to revenues if the firm priced all its products at marginal cost. Multiproduct scale economies can also be expressed as a function of economies of scope and product-specific economies (see Baumol, Panzar, and Willig, *Contestable Markets*).

Table 2-5. Multiproduct Scale Elasticities, Overall Scope Economies, and Productivity for U.S. and Japanese Automakers, Selected Years, 1970–83

| | Multiproduct scale elasticities | | Overall scope economies[a] | | Productivity | | | |
| | | | | | United States | | Japan | |
Year	United States	Japan	United States	Japan	Thousands of dollars	Percent	Thousands of yen	Percent
1970	1.22	1.12	0.109	0.439	63,982	0.398	−2,604,482	−0.675
1975	0.88	1.10	−0.513	0.370	780	0.007	419,898	0.074
1980	0.98	1.09	−0.762	0.332	76,097	0.776	2,038,547	0.003
1981	1.08	1.08	−0.867	0.304	107,072	1.230	3,340,581	0.396
1982	1.12	1.07	−0.742	0.330	69,862	0.755	3,281,135	0.358
1983	1.12	n.a.	−0.367	n.a.	74,485	0.465	n.a.	n.a.
Sample means	1.03	1.09	0.065	0.696	90,236	0.519	526,594	0.081

Sources: Authors' calculations based on sources in appendix B to this chapter.
n.a. Not available.
a. Scope economies are evaluated at zero output levels. The basic results were not changed when the scope economies were evaluated at small output levels.

economies suggest that a firm should expand production; diseconomies suggest a firm should contract it. At the sample mean, the estimates indicate that both the U.S. and Japanese industries operate at slightly increasing returns. The Japanese economies of scale have remained fairly stable, but the recession of 1981–82 and the voluntary quotas in effect since 1981 have exacerbated the U.S. industry's inability to exhaust its economies of scale and operate at the minimum point of long-run total cost (chapter 3 shows that quotas actually caused U.S. automakers to reduce production).

The inefficiencies in the scale of U.S. firms' operations could be related to the scope of those operations. Economies of scope measure the percentage cost savings due to joint production. Cost savings will be positive in the presence of economies of joint production and negative in the presence of diseconomies of joint production.[18] Table 2-5 estimates scope economies for both industries. The results indicate that at the sample means both industries experience economies of joint production, with the Japanese experiencing the greater economies. However, since 1975 the U.S. industry has suffered from diseconomies of scope, which peaked in 1981, while during the same period the Japanese industry has enjoyed fairly stable economies of scope. One explanation is that

18. Economies of scope are defined as $S_c = [C(Y_T) + C(Y_{N-T}) - C(Y_N)]/C(Y_N)$, where T and $N - T$ represent disjoint groups of the output set that collectively account for all output $N [T \cup (N - T) = N]$. Thus $C(Y_T)$ and $C(Y_{N-T})$ respectively represent the costs of producing output set T and output set $N - T$ independently, while $C(Y_N)$ represents the cost of producing them jointly.

Japanese firms can produce different sizes of vehicles, including trucks, on the same production line. This is less true for U.S. automakers because the sizes of their vehicles vary too greatly. In addition, after 1975 Japanese automakers pioneered the use of robotic welding, which increased the flexibility of their production lines; U.S. automakers did not begin to invest in robotics on a significant scale until the 1980s.[19] Overall, this comparison of U.S. and Japanese technology suggests that lower Japanese production costs may to a small degree be explained by their more efficient scale and scope of operations.

Differences in overall productivity growth, especially in labor productivity, are widely believed to be another important explanation for the cost differential. Table 2-5 shows the estimated percentage change in total costs for Japanese and U.S. automakers from 1970 to 1983. Productivity increases when costs fall. It decreases if costs rise.[20] At the sample mean, neither industry experienced significant productivity growth. Japanese automakers maintained fairly small productivity changes in 1982, while by 1983 the U.S. firms reached levels of productivity change that converged with those of the Japanese firms.[21] Thus it appears

19. Kenneth Flamm, "International Differences in Industrial Robot Use: Trends, Puzzles, and Possible Implications for Developing Countries," World Bank discussion paper, report DRD 185 (Washington, D.C., July 1986).

20. Estimates of each industry's productivity growth are obtained by differentiating the estimated cost functions with respect to time and calculating the following expression:

$$\frac{\partial C}{\partial T} = \delta + D(T - \overline{T}) + \sum_i F_i(Y_i - \overline{Y_i}) + \sum_j G_j(W_j - \overline{W_j}).$$

Thus, δ represents productivity growth, all variables held at their sample mean. Productivity growth estimates at points other than the sample means are obtained by using the complete equation. Because this equation represents the pure productivity effect, productivity growth can be said to have occurred only if $\partial C/\partial T$ is negative. Attempts were made to control for the effect of product quality and automobile regulations on productivity, but the hedonic attributes that controlled for product quality and a regulation variable (defined as the percentage reduction in the emissions level mandated for each year) were statistically insignificant.

21. The statistical imprecision of the time coefficient makes it difficult to draw firm conclusions regarding the sign and the magnitude of the changes in productivity. However, the key finding for our purposes, which is likely to be reliable, is that U.S.-Japanese productivity growth is similar. Indeed, using a different approach, Melvyn Fuss and Leonard Waverman found at their sample mean that the rate of technical change (as measured by research and development expenditures instead of a time variable) is not significantly different in the United States and Japan. See "Productivity Growth in the Automobile Industry, 1970–1980: A Comparison of Canada, Japan, and the United States," paper prepared for the National Bureau of Economic Research, August 1985.

that improvements in U.S. productivity growth are partly responsible for the recent reduction in the marginal cost differential.

Previous studies have suggested that differences in labor productivity contribute substantially to the cost differential. For example, Abernathy, Clark, and Kantrow estimate that U.S. automakers require 1.88 times the labor required by the Japanese firms to produce the same output; the National Academy of Engineering's estimate is 1.77.[22] Our data yield an estimate of 2.20. However, all these figures are misleading because they fail adequately to control for differences in vertical integration and product mix and scale.[23] For example, nearly 37 percent of Japanese automakers' production consists of vehicles—minicars and motorcycles—much smaller than any that U.S. automakers produce. When we simulate differences in labor productivity controlling for differences in vertical integration, production scale, and product mix, we find that Japanese labor is 1.36 times more productive than U.S. labor.[24] Labor productivity differences do exist and contribute to the cost differential, but not nearly so much as has been previously suggested.

Achieving Cost Competitiveness

Although as of 1982 there was a cost differential between U.S. and Japanese cars, the causes do not completely agree with conventional

22. William Abernathy, Kim Clark, and Alan Kantrow, *Industrial Renaissance: Producing a Competitive Future for America* (Basic Books, 1983); and National Academy of Engineering, *The Competitive Status of the U.S. Auto Industry* (Washington, D.C.: National Academy Press, 1982).

23. Our estimate of relative labor productivity makes no correction for product mix and scale, while the estimates of the National Academy of Engineering and Abernathy, Clark, and Kantrow make ad hoc corrections based on accounting data. Another procedure would be to compare the higher-order coefficients in the cost function that give estimates of the marginal productivity of labor. But this procedure compares marginal productivities without controlling for differences in production scale and mix or for differences in firms' vertical integration. In effect, one is simply comparing firms' labor requirements for different outputs and production practices.

24. This result is obtained by assuming that firms produce at the 1982 output mix of General Motors, which is at a scale close to Ford's 1982 output (1,030,386 vehicles). Simulations that made different assumptions regarding the scale and mix of output did not lead to substantially different estimates of the labor productivity differential. If labor productivity is measured in worker-hours instead of workers, all of the labor productivity figures cited above fall by roughly 15 percent because Japanese workers work more hours a week than American workers.

Table 2-6. Changes in U.S.-Japanese Marginal Cost Differential for Small Cars under Alternative Production, Wage, and Exchange Rate Scenarios
1975 dollars at 1982 exchange rates unless otherwise indicated

Scenario	Manufacturing costs		Tariffs and transport costs (Japan only)	Difference
	United States	Japan		
Base case	3,336	1,739	296	1,301
	Changes in industry behavior			
U.S. firms increase production by 20 percent	2,718	1,739	296	683
U.S. firms produce at Nissan's output mix	2,887	1,739	296	852
U.S. firms equal labor productivity of Japanese firms at all stages of production	3,183	1,739	296	1,148
U.S. firms pay 1982 average Japanese industry wages ($11,227 in 1975 dollars)	2,215	1,739	296	180
	Changes in government policy			
Exchange rate of 167.5 yen to the dollar	3,336	2,585	296	455
Exchange rate of 167.5 yen to the dollar, and U.S. firms pay 1982 average Japanese industry wages ($11,227 in 1975 dollars)	2,215	2,585	296	−666

Source: Authors' calculations based on sources in appendix B to this chapter.

wisdom. On average in the period 1965 to 1982, differences in the cost of funds were not a factor. Labor productivity differences, while significant, were not nearly so great as previously argued. But the relative cost of labor was significant because the average Japanese worker's earnings were roughly 60 percent of a U.S. worker's earnings. Finally, differences in the scale and scope of operations also contributed to the cost differential.

How can U.S. automakers reduce this differential? How can the government help?

Automakers can increase production to exhaust economies of scale, produce a mix of vehicles that yields economies of joint production, improve labor productivity, and reduce labor costs. Table 2-6 shows the results of a simulation of each of these changes given a base case of 1982 values of the cost and output variables (measured in 1975 dollars).[25]

25. The 1982 exchange rate was 249.05 yen to the dollar. The 1986 exchange rate is

Each scenario represents an independent change from the base case. Either a 20 percent increase in U.S. auto production or a change to a vehicle mix resembling that of a representative Japanese firm (that is, a shift toward producing more small cars) decreases the cost differential by some $500 from that of the base case. Unfortunately, changes in output and mix may not be practical because they are constrained by demand. Even if a change were practical, the remaining differential would still be about $700.

If U.S. labor productivity at all stages of production (in-house and at earlier stages) equaled Japan's, a $153 reduction in the cost differential could be expected. Although this represents only a 10 percent reduction from eliminating a substantially greater labor productivity differential, it is important to bear in mind that labor costs constitute 41 percent of total costs when all stages of production are taken into account.[26]

A significant decrease in the cost differential could be achieved by equating U.S. and Japanese wages—that is, by cutting U.S. autoworkers' wages by 41 percent. Although such cuts per se are out of the question, U.S. automakers have recently begun to reduce labor costs by increasing imports of foreign manufactured parts and in some cases complete vehicles. Because vehicle assembly is not the only point at which labor costs are incurred, American producers can reduce a vehicle's labor costs by building its components abroad, thus taking advantage of lower foreign wages, and assembling it in the United States.[27]

In addition to the direct reductions in costs that the U.S. industry can achieve through more efficient operations, the government can affect the cost differential through economic policy—directly by influencing

---

used in our simulation of the effects of government policy. The use of different annual values for cost and output variables did not lead to any significant changes in the results.

26. This cost figure is based on General Motors' 1982 production activity.

27. This is called modular assembly. The top tier of suppliers delivers modules such as an instrument panel or front suspension. The parts that make up the module come largely from abroad. Thus, fewer and larger sections of a car are joined together in assembly plants, rather than putting thousands of parts together on a traditional assembly line. Given increased competition in the small car market provided by Hyundai and increased competition in upscale autos provided by Japanese automakers (for instance, Honda's new Acura line), U.S. producers will likely accelerate their use of modular assembly, subject to conditions imposed by labor contracts and inventory logistics. And if the yen continues its strength against the dollar, U.S. firms will probably rely more heavily on Mexico, Brazil, or Korea instead of Japan to carry out modular assembly. See Al Fleming, "Modular Assembly Called Key to Survival," *Automotive News,* August 4, 1986.

exchange rates and the cost of funds and indirectly by mitigating the cost to autoworkers of making the U.S. industry more competitive.[28]

During the late 1970s and early 1980s, high U.S. interest rates, caused by the tight credit policies of the Federal Reserve Bank and by increased government borrowing to cover the budget deficit, artificially increased the value of the dollar and weakened U.S. industry competitiveness. Since the spring of 1985, however, the yen has appreciated substantially against the dollar. From spring 1985 to spring 1986 the exchange rate fell from 240 yen to the dollar to 165 to the dollar. At the 1986 Tokyo economic summit the participating nations agreed to a system of managed floating exchange rates but gave no indication that the new dollar-yen exchange rate was out of line with economic reality.[29] This view was reaffirmed at U.S.-Japanese trade discussions held in October 1986.

Government policy influences the cost of funds through interest rates and corporate taxation. Recent Federal Reserve policies have contributed to a fall in interest rates, and in 1986 Congress passed a tax reform bill that will reduce the maximum corporate tax rate from 46 percent to 34 percent but eliminate the investment tax credit. The net effect of these changes may be to lower the cost of funds for the automobile industry.[30]

In table 2-6 we simulate the effects of lower exchange rates and a lower cost of funds on the marginal cost differential. The results indicate that at an exchange rate of 167.5 yen to the dollar the marginal cost differential is cut by roughly two-thirds from what it is under the base case.[31] The cost differential is eliminated at an exchange rate of 151.9

28. Because automobile safety and emissions regulations apply to American and Japanese vehicles alike, government policy that changes these regulations is not likely to affect the cost differential significantly.

29. Under a system of managed floating exchange rates, rates are not fixed, but their variation is to be limited by adjusting the basic mechanics of the economy. See Peter T. Kilborn, "The Float, and How to Manage It," *New York Times,* May 11, 1986.

30. Because sales prospects are currently favorable, auto manufacturers are confident they will prosper under the new tax code. But if the industry encounters a prolonged period of poor sales, it will be hurt because under the new law it will lose tax incentives that formerly helped write off losses. See Geoff Sundstrom, "How Tax Bill Would Affect Auto Industry," *Automotive News,* August 25, 1986.

31. It is estimated that roughly 15 percent of the cost of manufacturing a Japanese vehicle is imported (that is, not determined by the yen). Thus our simulations represent the maximum change in Japanese costs resulting from changes in exchange rates. See James Trask, "Exchange Rates and the Cost of Japanese Cars," paper presented at the International Atlantic Economic Conference, Montreal, Canada, October 1984.

yen to the dollar, which is a plausible equilibrium value.[32] A modest reduction in the cost of funds does not contribute significantly to reducing the cost differential.[33] Finally, equating U.S. and Japanese wage rates at the 1986 exchange rate of 167.5 yen to the dollar would actually give the U.S. industry a cost advantage. A 17 percent reduction in U.S. wages at this exchange rate eliminates any cost differential.

Recent government and industry policy appears to be eliminating the U.S.-Japanese cost differential, although at a cost of increased unemployment among autoworkers. Because greater reliance on foreign manufactured components reduces the amount of automobile-related employment in the United States, adjustments will have to be made by displaced U.S. workers.[34] The trade adjustment assistance (TAA) program, established in the Trade Act of 1974, was designed to provide compensation, retraining, and employment assistance to workers whose employment was adversely affected by increasing levels of imports.[35] There is some question whether in practice the TAA program contributed to adjustment, and its appropriations were sharply cut back in 1982.[36] To be sure, workers want trade protection, not an employment adjustment program. But given this political reality, a TAA program that provides actual adjustment assistance could be justified on grounds of efficiency as being superior to protectionist legislation. In addition, an effective program would reduce friction between management and labor by easing the adjustment some workers will have to make, although such a program would aid only currently employed workers.

Finally, government policy must recognize that cost competitiveness

32. Lawrence B. Krause raises the possibility of an equilibrium exchange rate of 100 yen to the dollar. See "Does a Yen Valued at 100 per Dollar Make Any Sense?" (unpublished paper, Brookings, January 1986).

33. Because this finding is based on a statistically insignificant coefficient (the output–user cost of capital interaction parameter), we do not report a numerical value.

34. The magnitude of this adjustment depends on how quickly U.S. companies reduce their work force through the use of modular assembly as opposed to attrition. Ford and General Motors have announced they plan to reduce their work force during the remainder of the decade by not replacing retiring autoworkers. In addition, General Motors has offered new incentives for certain white-collar employees to resign and recently announced plans to close eleven plants and lay off 29,000 workers.

35. For a full discussion of the trade adjustment assistance program, see Department of Labor, Bureau of International Affairs, *United States–Japan Comparative Study of Employment Adjustment* (Department of Labor, March 1985).

36. See Harry C. Katz, *Shifting Gears: Changing Labor Relations in the U.S. Automobile Industry* (Cambridge, Mass.: MIT Press, 1985).

is at hand.[37] Thus it should not support auto manufacturers' joint ventures or consolidations or revive trade protection on the grounds that such actions are needed to achieve cost competitiveness. U.S. automobile firms should be forced to compete under unrestricted market conditions.

Appendix A: Specification and Estimation of Cost Functions

The multiproduct cost function used in this analysis can be written as $C = C(Y,W,T)$, where C represents total costs, Y_i is the physical level of output i, W is the vector of factor prices, and T is the time variable. To estimate this function, we specify a quadratic approximation, which represents a second-order Taylor's approximation around the mean. The estimated cost function is thus written as

$$
(2\text{-}1) \quad C = \alpha_o + \sum_i \alpha_i (Y_i - \overline{Y}_i) + \sum_j \beta_j (W_j - \overline{W}_j) + \delta (T - \overline{T})
$$

$$
+ \tfrac{1}{2} \left[\sum_i \sum_m A_{im}(Y_i - \overline{Y}_i)(Y_m - \overline{Y}_m) \right.
$$

$$
+ \sum_j \sum_n B_{jn}(W_j - \overline{W}_j)(W_n - \overline{W}_n) + \left. D (T - \overline{T})^2 \right]
$$

$$
+ \sum_i \sum_j E_{ij}(Y_i - \overline{Y}_i)(W_j - \overline{W}_j)
$$

$$
+ \sum_i F_i (Y_i - \overline{Y}_i)(T - \overline{T}) + \sum_j G_j (W_j - \overline{W}_j)(T - \overline{T}) + \epsilon,
$$

where A_{im} equals A_{mi} for every i,m; B_{jn} equals B_{nj} for every n,j; and ϵ represents a disturbance term.

37. Our estimate of the marginal cost differential does not consider further appreciation of the yen against the dollar or reductions in labor costs because of outsourcing (modular assembly) that have occurred since 1982. Thus the current marginal cost differential is likely to be negligible, even if one anticipates possible help that Japanese companies may receive from their government. See John Holusha, "Yen's Rise Forcing Toyota to Trim Sails," *New York Times,* November 10, 1986.

The corresponding factor demand equation for the *j*th factor can be derived by Shepherd's lemma,

$$X_j = \frac{\partial C}{\partial W_j} = \beta_j + \sum_n B_{jn}(W_n - \overline{W}_n) + \sum_i E_i(Y_i - \overline{Y}_i) + G_{jT}(T - \overline{T}) + \epsilon_j,$$

where ϵ_j represents the disturbance term. Because the error terms of the cost and factor demand equations are correlated and there are common parameters across equations, it is desirable to estimate the factor demand equations jointly with the cost function to increase the efficiency of the estimates.

Joint estimation of the cost function and the factor demand equations was achieved by Zellner's seemingly unrelated regression procedure. The outputs were instrumented to account for endogeneity,[38] and the covariance matrix was estimated using a procedure developed by Halbert White to account for the presence of heteroskedasticity.[39] Estimates of the complete set of parameters are set out in tables 2-7 and 2-8.

Appendix B: Data Description and Construction of Variables

In this appendix we discuss the American data base and then its Japanese counterpart. In constructing the data, we have tried to use definitions that are as comparable as possible (various accounting practices such as methods of depreciation and amortization did not vary significantly between the two countries). The basic data collection scheme follows Friedlaender, Winston, and Wang, but considerable effort has been made to overcome acknowledged deficiencies in this earlier sample.[40]

38. A description of the instruments is contained in appendix B to this chapter. Based on a Hausman specification test, we found that the null hypothesis of output exogeneity was rejected for all U.S. and Japanese firms except Chrysler. See Jerry A. Hausman, "Specification Tests in Econometrics," *Econometrica,* vol. 46 (November 1978), pp. 1251–71.

39. Halbert White, "A Heteroskedasticity-Consistent Covariance Matrix Estimator and a Direct Test for Heteroskedasticity," *Econometrica,* vol. 48 (May 1980), pp. 817–38.

40. See "Costs, Technology, and Productivity in the U.S. Automobile Industry."

Table 2-7. Estimated Coefficients of U.S. Quadratic Cost Function

Variable	Coefficient[a]	Standard error[b]	Variable	Coefficient[a]	Standard error[b]
Constant	17,368,530	335,373	W_{km}	34,701.53	8,183.48
Y_s (small car)	3.414	1.519	$W_l Y_s$	0.141	0.028
Y_l (large car)	5.010	0.394	$W_l Y_l$	0.137	0.006
Y_t (truck)	9.395	1.395	$W_l Y_t$	−0.024	0.031
Y_{ss}	−0.00000193	0.00000153	$W_k Y_s$	−0.015	0.025
Y_{ll}	0.000000857	0.000000171	$W_k Y_l$	0.022	0.005
Y_{tt}	0.00000508	0.00000182	$W_k Y_t$	0.045	0.022
Y_{sl}	0.00000142	0.000000322	$W_m Y_s$	0.901	0.854
Y_{st}	−0.00000358	0.00000144	$W_m Y_l$	3.329	0.197
Y_{lt}	−0.00000169	0.000000471	$W_m Y_t$	9.986	0.884
W_k (capital)	113,271.5	5,524.0	T (time)	90,236.44	60,121.7
W_l (labor)	279,656.8	5,119.41	TY_s	0.220	0.076
W_m (material)	13,009,212	159,824	TY_l	−0.002	0.023
W_{ll}	−5,113.87	2,239.25	TY_t	−0.153	0.103
W_{lk}	1,528.49	379.05	TW_l	4,764.09	1,522.61
W_{lm}	−6,483.76	29,404.2	TW_k	−374.70	935.75
W_{kk}	−3,665.44	491.139	TW_m	57,654.73	37,794.6
W_{mm}	−980,550	1,012,493	TT	−16,298.70	6,413.73

a. R^2 cost equation is .966; R^2 labor equation is .949; R^2 capital equation is .569; R^2 materials equation is .96.

b. Asymptotic White heteroskedastic-consistent standard errors.

The United States

The data base for the United States is a pooled, cross-section time series sample of the Big Three domestic automobile manufacturers for 1955–83. Although the organizational structures of the companies are different, Friedlaender, Winston, and Wang found that their production technologies were sufficiently similar to analyze them as if they shared a common technology.

COSTS OF DOMESTIC PRODUCTION. The dependent variable of the cost equation should measure the total cost of domestic production of automobiles. However, available data do not make the distinction of location and type of goods produced because financial reports for the three U.S. firms present data on a consolidated basis. No adjustment is made in this analysis to account for automotive versus nonautomotive production. Although all the automobile firms produce other goods (from kitchen appliances to aircraft engines), nonautomotive operations make up only a small percentage of total operations. For example, nonautomotive sales constituted only 4 percent of General Motors' total sales in 1983, and only 8 percent of Ford's total sales.[41]

The distinction between domestic and foreign operations appears

41. *Value Line Investment Survey*, September 28, 1984.

Table 2-8. Estimated Coefficients of Japanese Quadratic Cost Function

Variable	Coefficient[a]	Standard error[b]	Variable	Coefficient[a]	Standard error[b]
Constant	647,887,865	7,455,717	W_{mm}	−307.538	139.682
Y_c (motorcycle)	67.536	9.697	$W_k Y_c$	0.124	0.050
Y_m (minicar)	278.874	86.796	$W_k Y_m$	0.229	0.559
Y_s (small car)	554.171	24.009	$W_k Y_s$	0.807	0.185
Y_l (large car)	572.323	324.533	$W_k Y_l$	−2.633	2.321
Y_t (truck)	2,242.696	180.625	$W_k Y_t$	3.615	1.478
Y_{cc}	0.00000497	0.00000387	$W_l Y_c$	−0.0001999	0.0006636
Y_{cm}	0.00000380	0.0000122	$W_l Y_m$	−0.023	0.006
Y_{cs}	−0.0000228	0.00000779	$W_l Y_s$	0.016	0.002
Y_{mm}	−0.0000399	0.000141	$W_l Y_l$	0.007	0.026
Y_{ms}	−0.0000804	0.0000823	$W_l Y_t$	−0.025	0.016
Y_{mt}	0.00271	0.000570	$W_m Y_c$	0.383	0.019
Y_{ss}	−0.0000157	0.0000112	$W_m Y_m$	1.439	0.177
Y_{sl}	0.0000159	0.000104	$W_m Y_s$	2.599	0.064
Y_{st}	−0.000114	0.0000604	$W_m Y_l$	3.202	0.842
Y_{ll}	0.000370	0.001685	$W_m Y_t$	10.062	0.520
Y_{lt}	0.000772	0.001019	T (time)	526,593.50	1,776,497
Y_{tt}	−0.000464	0.000801	TY_c	1.491	0.408
W_k (capital)	947,747.30	57,267.20	TY_m	−4.217	3.769
W_l (labor)	23,782.82	601.728	TY_s	0.231	0.547
W_m (material)	2,832,482	22,138.10	TY_l	20.463	7.242
W_{kk}	−12,356.4	1,756.87	TY_t	−17.159	6.536
W_{kl}	115.839	21.979	TW_k	−37,506.7	14,264.2
W_{km}	874.788	428.145	TW_l	383.432	191.186
W_{ll}	−2.296	0.561	TW_m	4,917.064	4,412.86
W_{lm}	−5.740	6.147	TT	422,480.6	111,851.0

a. R^2 cost equation is .994; R^2 labor equation is .928; R^2 capital equation is .789; R^2 materials equation is .996.
b. Asymptotic White heteroskedastic-consistent standard errors.

more important. Ford, historically the most involved in foreign production, earned from 11 percent to 75 percent of its net income from foreign production between 1958 and 1983; its domestic sales accounted for 22 percent to 51 percent of worldwide sales.[42] Such figures vary not only over time but also among firms.

It is difficult to construct a cost variable that excludes the costs of foreign production. Usually, total cost, $\overline{C}$, is defined as the sum of costs of all inputs, in this case, capital, labor, and materials, so that

$$(2\text{-}2) \qquad \overline{C} = P_k K + P_l L + P_m M,$$

where P_k, P_l, and P_m are input prices and K, L, and M the units of capital, labor, and materials used. First each component of cost is constructed, and the sum is defined as costs. To exclude the costs of foreign operations would require data on each component broken down into domestic and foreign costs. Although it is possible to construct variables for the

42. Telephone conversation with Dennis Fogel of Ford Motor Company on January 15, 1985.

material and labor components that exclude foreign operations, capital costs are only reported on a consolidated basis. This makes it impossible to estimate domestic costs for each firm without making some assumptions about the relative magnitudes of domestic and foreign capital costs.

Nevertheless, by using the firms' financial data on domestic operations, it is possible to obtain an indirect measure of the costs of domestic production. We begin by using the identity that total sales revenues must equal the sum of economic costs plus economic profits. Thus

$$(2\text{-}3) \qquad\qquad S = \overline{C} + \Pi,$$

where S, $\overline{C}$, and Π represent sales, economic costs, and economic profit, respectively. The financial statements of the automobile firms provide data on "net sales" and "before-tax net earnings" (hereafter, net earnings).[43] Using this data we can obtain estimates of domestic costs as

$$(2\text{-}4) \qquad\qquad \overline{C} = S - NE + DIV,$$

where NE represents net earnings and DIV represents dividends, and net sales, net earnings, and dividends are for domestic operations alone (unfortunately, data on dividends paid are available only for worldwide operations). The link between equation 2-4 and equation 2-3 lies in the relationship between economic profit, net earnings, and dividends. Accounting relationships allocate net earnings between dividends and retained earnings, RE, and use the identity

$$(2\text{-}5) \qquad\qquad NE = DIV + RE.$$

Thus if we assume that retained earnings approximate economic profits,[44] then we can substitute Π for RE in equation 2-5 and write

$$(2\text{-}6) \qquad\qquad \Pi = NE - DIV.$$

Substituting this expression into equation 2-3 yields equation 2-4, which

43. The accounting definitions for these terms are given in Howard S. Noble, *Accounting Principles*, 5th ed. (Cincinnati: Southwestern Publishing, 1949). Net sales equal gross sales less returns and allowances. Net earnings equal net sales less cost of goods sold less operating expenses plus other income less expenses.

44. The implications of this assumption are that domestic costs may be overstated because of the inclusion of additional overhead. However, this inclusion represents a very small fraction of total costs. As a partial check on whether the capital component of total costs seriously affected the results, we eliminated capital costs from total costs and estimated a "variable cost" system. We found that our primary conclusions were basically unchanged even when we eliminated the user cost of capital from the set of explanatory variables.

permits us to calculate the costs of domestic production from available financial data.[45]

CAPITAL. The total cost of capital is obtained as a residual using equation 2-2. Capital costs, which include interest expenses, dividends, depreciation, and amortization, are then divided by the user cost of capital, described below, to obtain the dependent variable K, which is expressed in units of capital consumed.[46] As discussed previously, this capital variable may also include other expenses that ideally would not be included as capital. The most significant of these is likely to be nonautomotive costs, which will be included as capital costs because the labor and material cost variables relate only to automotive costs.

The user cost of capital is calculated using the analysis in Boadway and Wildasin and represents the cost to firms of holding and using assets during a period of time.[47] The four components of the user cost of capital are the cost of financing the asset, depreciation, capital gains or losses, and any tax savings to the firm from holding the asset.

The firm is assumed to be a profit maximizer in perfectly competitive capital markets; that is, the firm adjusts its holdings of capital assets to equate the marginal benefit of an additional increment of capital (value of marginal product of capital) with the marginal cost of holding the assets.

45. The financial data required to calculate the domestic production costs were obtained as follows: for Ford, Dennis Fogel in the Office of Investor Relations provided data on domestic net sales and net earnings during a phone conversation in January 1985; for Chrysler, E. S. Harris, manager of external reporting and consolidation provided similar data in a letter dated May 14, 1985; for General Motors, domestic net sales and net earnings were computed using ratios of U.S. to total sales and earnings provided in Standard and Poor's *Standard Corporate Descriptions*. Total sales and earnings data were also obtained from Standard and Poor. U.S. sales and earnings were then calculated using the following identities: total sales × (U.S. sales/total sales) = U.S. sales; and total earnings × (U.S. earnings/total earnings) = U.S. earnings. Finally, U.S. costs for each firm were defined as U.S. sales less U.S. earnings plus dividends.

46. Although it appears possible to use K as an argument in a short-run cost function, which could be used to derive a long-run cost function, doing so would be inadvisable because of possible measurement errors in K. These measurement errors pose fewer problems when K is a dependent variable.

47. Robin W. Boadway and David E. Wildasin, *Public Sector Economics*, 2d ed. (Boston: Little Brown, 1984), pp. 321–47. Admittedly, there is some inconsistency between a neoclassical construction of the user cost of capital and a total cost variable that assumes retained earnings approximate economic profits. However, given that the measurement error caused by this assumption is not likely to bias the estimated coefficients, it is appropriate to follow established theoretical guidelines in constructing the user cost of capital rather than to modify the construction of the user cost to be completely consistent with the construction of total cost.

Given these assumptions, and further assuming that firms take taxes, capital gains, and inflation into account, one can define the user cost of capital, P_k, as

$$(2\text{-}7) \qquad P_k = q \, \frac{\bar{r} + \delta - g}{1 - u} \, (1 - \phi) \left(1 - \frac{u\alpha}{r + \alpha} \right),$$

where q is the purchase price of one unit of capital, $\bar{r}$ is the real cost of financing, r is the nominal cost of financing ($\bar{r} + \pi^e$, where π^e is the expected inflation rate), δ is the economic depreciation rate, u is the corporate income tax rate, ϕ is investment tax credit, α is the reported depreciation rate, and g is capital gains on the firm's assets.

To interpret this expression,[48] it is useful to look at the marginal condition satisfied when the firm has chosen the optimal capital stock:

$$(2\text{-}8) \quad (1 - u)P \cdot MP_k = (q\bar{r} + q\delta - qg)\,(1 - \phi) \left(1 - \frac{u\alpha}{r + \alpha} \right).$$

The left side is the marginal benefit of obtaining another unit of capital: $P \cdot MP_k$ is the value of marginal product of capital, and the first term $(1 - u)$ adjusts this to reflect corporate tax payments on revenues generated by the sale of output.

On the right side, $q\bar{r}$ is the cost of financing one unit of capital, $q\delta$ is the dollar economic depreciation on one unit of capital, and qg is the capital gain on assets. The first term on the right side $(q\bar{r} + q\delta - qg)$ is thus the simple user cost of capital when factors such as inflation and taxes are ignored.

But because firms are also given tax credits for each dollar they invest, the cost of capital is adjusted to reflect this with ϕ in the second term.

The third term on the right side adjusts for the fact that firms are allowed to write off the reported depreciation on their assets. It can be shown that $\alpha/(r + \alpha)$ is the present value of future depreciation write-offs. Given this, $u\alpha/(r + \alpha)$ is the present value of these tax savings on one dollar of capital. This third term thus reduces the cost of capital by the present value of these tax savings.

If one divides both sides of equation 2-8 by $(1 - u)$, the

48. In its early years, 1972–73, the investment tax credit was of the type that reduced the depreciation base. For these years, the relevant formula for the user cost of capital is

$$P_k = q \, \frac{\bar{r} + \delta - g}{1 - u} \left(1 - \phi - 1 - \frac{u\alpha}{r + \alpha} \right).$$

right side may be interpreted as the user cost of capital, which is the expression in equation 2-7.

Ideally, one would like firm-specific measures of each of these variables. The purchase price of capital, for example, will vary depending on the type of capital (equipment, structures, and so forth). To the extent that the types of capital typically held by firms in this study differ, one would need different prices for each firm. Unfortunately, this information is difficult to obtain. In some cases, the best data to be found are industry-specific (as for automobiles); in others, only national data (as for manufacturing) are available. Nevertheless, it is likely that there is not a great deal of firm-specific variation among the variables.[49]

COST OF FINANCING. The cost of financing is computed as a weighted average of the cost of borrowing and the cost of equity, where the cost of equity is estimated using a capital-asset pricing model. These calculations yield a variable that represents the minimum required after-tax return on capital to investors of the firm.

The capital-asset pricing model defines the cost of equity to firms as $K_{ei} = r_f + \beta_i (r_m - r_f)$, where K_{ei} is the cost of equity, r_f is the risk-free rate of return, r_m is the expected return on stocks, and β_i is a measure of the riskiness of firm i's stock.[50] Thus by using the appropriate data, one can obtain estimates of the cost of equity.[51]

49. The sources of these data are as follows: the variable, q, is represented by the implicit price deflator on fixed nonresidential investment found in U.S. Department of Commerce, Bureau of Labor Statistics, *Business Statistics*. Calculations for the economic depreciation rate, δ, for American corporations are given in Hatsopoulos, "High Cost of Capital," p. 101. The corporate income tax rate, u, for firms in the motor vehicles industry is calculated as total taxes divided by income subject to tax for that industry. Data were obtained from U.S. Department of Treasury, Internal Revenue Service, *Statistics of Income: Business Tax Returns*, various years. The investment tax credit, θ, for equipment was taken from Hatsopoulos, "High Cost of Capital," p. 97. The reported depreciation rate, α, is calculated as the ratio of reported depreciation to book value of depreciable assets for the motor vehicles industry. Data for this calculation are given in U.S. Department of Treasury, Internal Revenue Service, *Statistics of Income: Business Tax Returns*. The rate of capital gains, g, is calculated as the percentage change in q. The calculations and sources for the cost of financing, $r, \bar{r}$, are described below.

50. This is the standard finance textbook formula used to calculate the cost of equity. See, for example, Richard Brealey and Stewart Myers, *Principles of Corporate Finance*, 2d ed. (McGraw-Hill, 1984). This text was used as the source of this and other finance-related formulas.

51. The data used to estimate the cost of equity were obtained as follows: the risk-free rate of return is defined as the yield on U.S. three-month treasury bills from *Business Statistics*. The difference between the market and risk-free rates of return (the

The after-tax cost of capital is obtained by weighting the cost of equity and the cost of borrowing by their relative importance in the firm's financing portfolio. It can be obtained by

$$(2\text{-}9) \qquad \bar{r} = K_i(1 - u)\frac{B}{B + E} + \left(\frac{K_e}{(1 - \theta)} \cdot \frac{E}{B + E}\right) - \pi^e,$$

where $\bar{r}$ is the cost of financing assets, K_i is the cost of borrowing, K_e is the cost of equity, u is the marginal corporate income tax rate, B is the market value of debt, E is the market value of equity, θ is the tax rate payable on equity income, and π^e is the expected inflation rate.[52]

This expression also includes adjustments for inflation and personal income taxes. Inflation is taken into account by adjusting $\bar{r}$, which represents the real cost of financing, for the expected inflation.[53] This adjustment is appropriate because it is likely that firms base their investment decisions on the real cost of financing, not on nominal values. Personal income taxes are an issue because the marginal individual buying equity from the firm will require a real return (net in the amount of taxes) equal to the cost of borrowing, K_i. Therefore to satisfy investors,

---

risk premium) was taken from calculations provided in R. G. Ibbotson and R. A. Sinquefield, *Stocks, Bonds, Bills and Inflation* (Charlottesville, Va.: Financial Analysts Research Foundation, 1982), p. 30. Asset betas were taken from *Value Line* for 1970–86 and from Friedlaender, Winston, and Wang, "Costs, Technology, and Productivity," for earlier years.

52. Data on dividend and retained earnings used to form these weights were obtained from Standard and Poor. The cost of borrowing was obtained from calculations in Ibbotson and Sinquefield, *Stocks.* The market value of debt, *B*, was obtained by multiplying the market-to-book ratio for bonds listed in the New York Stock Exchange, *NYSE Factbook, 1986,* by the book value of bonds as listed in Standard and Poor. And finally, the market value of equity was calculated by multiplying the average price of each firm's common stock, as shown in Standard and Poor, by the number of shares outstanding, as shown in *Value Line.*

53. The expected inflation series, π^e, was obtained by assuming that expectations are formed adaptively. Specifically, the expected inflation at time t is based on the actual inflation during year t and that of the preceding five years. The weights used for each year are current year, 0.34; current year − 1, 0.23; current year − 2, 0.17; current year − 3, 0.12; current year − 4, 0.08; current year − 5, 0.06, for a total of 1.00. These weights are determined by the relation,

$$\text{Weight}_t = .7^t/\Sigma.7^t.$$

This method for computing an expected inflation series was used in Hatsopoulos, "High Cost of Capital." Alternative assumptions about inflationary expectations did not affect the real cost of equity (Ibid., p. 53).

the before-tax payment by the firm must be $K_i /(1 - \theta)$, where θ is the appropriate tax rate paid by holders of the firm's stock.[54]

LABOR. Data on annual compensation for domestic employees of each of the Big Three automakers were obtained from the United Auto Workers. Data on the number of domestic employees were available from Moody's and Standard and Poor for Chrysler and Ford; General Motors provided data on its domestic employment.[55] The total labor cost for each firm was then obtained by multiplying the firm's compensation rate by its number of workers.

MATERIALS. Because data are not available on the cost of materials purchased by domestic plants, it is necessary to use total materials purchases by domestic operations. This is done by assuming that the ratio of domestic materials purchases to domestic sales is the same as the ratio of worldwide materials purchases to worldwide sales.[56]

Because the input demand equations utilize a measure of physical inputs, it is necessary to obtain a measure of real input usage. This can be done by dividing actual materials purchases by an appropriate price index. The nature of this price index, however, is a complicated issue

54. The appropriate tax rate paid by holders of a firm's stock is complicated because of the treatment of capital. Stockholders are subject to two types of taxes. Dividend payments are considered income and are taxed at the personal income tax rate, while capital gains from sales of stock whose price has risen are taxed differently depending on how long the stock has been held. If the holding period is less than one year, then short-term capital gains are taxed at the personal income tax rate. For our sample period, long-term capital gains are given preferential treatment in that only 40 percent of them are taxable. Capital losses (long-term or short-term) may be deducted from capital gains made from other stock sales. Given the difference in treatment of these earnings, the appropriate tax rate, θ, paid by a firm's stockholders can be represented by a weighted average of the two tax rates:

$$\theta = \frac{\text{dividends}}{\text{dividends} + \text{capital gains}} (t) + (0.4)(t) \frac{\text{capital gains}}{\text{dividends} + \text{capital gains}}.$$

To make this representation operational, it is assumed that increases in the retained earnings of a firm increase the value of the firm and thus give rise to capital gains. The weights actually used substitute retained earnings for capital gains in the above expression. The effects on taxes from capital losses are not dealt with here.

55. GM data were provided by John Harnett, General Motors Office of Public Relations, Washington, D.C.

56. To calculate domestic materials purchases we used $MP_d = (MP_w/S_w)S_d$, where MP represents materials purchases, S represents sales, and the subscripts d and w respectively represent domestic and worldwide values of the variables. Sales data are available from automakers' financial reports; materials purchases are available from their annual reports. This procedure is less tenable when outsourcing is considered, but outsourcing was not prevalent until after the period covered by our sample.

that must take supplier relationships into account. This problem is particularly important in dealing with U.S. and Japanese automobile costs because the relationships of automakers and suppliers in the two countries are very different.

In existing cost studies, composite materials price indexes have been constructed using a weighted sum of the prices of the major commodities used in production, while the relevant weights have been based on materials purchased. Although this approach is appealing because the requisite data are readily available, it is restrictive because it implicitly assumes that firms are fully vertically integrated. This assumption may be reasonable for U.S. automobile producers, but it is not consistent with observed automaker-supplier relationships in Japan.

The problem arises because the materials price index typically includes variables such as iron, steel, and glass. However, producers often purchase commodities such as engines, chassis, and finished windshields, each of which may contain a high component of labor costs, and a price index based on materials purchases can be seriously misleading. This condition suggests that in deriving a materials price index physical units are preferable to purchases as weights. Data in physical units, however, are not usually available. Nevertheless, if pounds of materials are directly translated into pounds of vehicles, then by dividing the aggregate cost of materials purchases by the total pounds of vehicles produced, it is possible to obtain a price equivalent to the one constructed for American firms. The major difference between these two approaches is that individual elements in the materials price index constructed using this approach cannot be identified.[57]

OUTPUT. To facilitate comparing Japanese and American cost structures, it is necessary to specify comparable classes of vehicles. Given the automobile classes for Japan, a sufficiently disaggregated output

---

57. To see this equivalence, note that the cost of materials is simply the sum of each input price times the quantity used of each input, or $\Sigma\, P_i \cdot Q_i$, where P_i is input i's price and Q_i represents the usage of material input i. Dividing this by pounds of materials ($\Sigma\, Q_i$), and rearranging, one obtains the price of materials: $P_m = \Sigma\, P_i\, (Q_i/\Sigma\, Q_i)$.

In this index each input price is weighted by the percentage of its content in the finished vehicle. This is, in principle, equivalent to a weighted price of materials. This procedure involves two assumptions: that pounds of materials are directly translated into pounds of vehicles and that the representative auto components given in *Wards Automobile Yearbook* are also applicable to trucks and buses. This latter assumption is not likely to hold, but since the output of trucks and buses is a relatively minor component of total output, the distortions caused by this assumption should be small.

series (including attributes for each model) for American automobiles would allow the definition of output classes for the U.S. firms to be nearly identical with the Japanese classes. To this end, production and specification data were collected for each of the U.S. firms.[58]

Given this output and specification data for each model, output classes were constructed with the specifications used by the Japanese. So, for example, if autos weighing more than 3,000 pounds are considered "standard" by the Japanese, all models produced by the American firms matching this specification were also labeled "standard." This approach led to two automobile classes for U.S. cars: small and large.[59]

INSTRUMENTS. The variables used to instrument a firm's output are its market share in the previous year, the absolute level of the particular output in the previous year, unemployment rate, installment credit outstanding, disposable personal income in constant dollars, population, GNP, prime rate, retail gas prices, and consumption per capita. The specification that is obtained by this procedure is basically an aggregate demand model for each type of vehicle. Changes in this specification did not significantly affect the estimation results. The market share for each firm was obtained from *Value Line*. The remaining variables were obtained from the *Survey of Current Business*, various issues.

Japan

The methodology for constructing the variables used in the Japanese automakers' cost function was similar to that used for American firms.

58. In addition, it is necessary to make adjustments so that consistency can be obtained between calendar years and model years. The problem arises because data on the number of autos produced are available by make (Chevrolet, Ford) for each calendar year but are only available by model (Chevette, Mustang) for each model year (twelve months ending October 31). Since annual production should be for the same time period as data used elsewhere in the cost function (calendar year), it is necessary to express the data as models in terms of calendar years. To this end it is assumed that the distribution of calendar year output within each make can be represented by the proportions given in the data for the model year. Thus if 1,000 Chevrolets were produced in calendar 1983, and one-fourth of Chevrolets in model year 1983 were Chevettes, it is assumed that 250 Chevettes were produced in calendar 1983. This figure is referred to as the calendar-year-equivalent output for a Chevette and was calculated for all models produced by each of the firms for the sample period.

59. Output and specification data were collected from various issues of *Automotive News*. Data on calendar year domestic truck production were available in *Wards Automobile Yearbook*. To calculate the average weight of trucks, truck production data tabulated by gross vehicle weight were used to construct a weighted average. These average weights were later used to calculate the number of pounds of trucks produced, one component of material costs.

This section describes the sources for the data used and any important differences in the methodology.

Although the distinction between foreign and domestic operations is important in the American firms, it is not necessary to adjust the Japanese data to exclude foreign operations because the financial data provided in the firms' annual reports exclude data on their foreign subsidiaries.

COST AND LABOR VARIABLES. Total cost, number of employees, and wages and benefits were obtained from an unpublished data set provided by the *Japan Economic Journal*. Average annual compensation was derived by dividing wages and benefits for all workers by the number of employees. Total cost is defined as the sum of capital, labor, and material costs. Descriptions of materials and capital costs are given below.

CAPITAL. To calculate the cost of capital for Japanese firms, we followed the analysis of Boadway and Wildasin, which we used to calculate the cost of capital for American firms.[60] The capital asset pricing model was used to calculate the cost of financing for Japanese firms. The methodology is the same as described earlier, except asset betas had to be calculated because they are not available.[61]

---

60. Boadway and Wildasin, *Public Sector Economics*. Sources for the variables used in the calculations (with the exception of the cost of financing, which is described separately below) are as follows: the price index for capital goods, q, is provided in Japanese Bureau of Statistics, *Japan Statistical Yearbook*, various issues. A proxy for economic depreciation, δ, is obtained from the *Japan Economic Journal* data base. A variable for actual depreciation based on engineering estimates rather than formulas used for tax purposes is divided by book value of depreciable assets also provided in *Japan Economic Journal*. The corporate income tax rate, u, is calculated for each firm by dividing total taxes by taxable income. Both variables were provided in *Japan Economic Journal*. The reported depreciation rate, α, is calculated as the ratio of reported depreciation to book value of depreciable assets for each firm. Both variables were obtained from the *Japan Economic Journal* data base. The percentage rate of change in the price index for capital goods, g, is provided in *Japan Statistical Yearbook*. The expected inflation rate, π^e, is calculated using the same method and parameters as for the United States.

The investment tax credit, ϕ, is assumed to be zero for Japanese firms. This assumption was also made in Hatsopoulos, "High Cost of Capital," primarily because such tax credits are scarce in Japan. This scarcity was verified in the description of the Japanese tax system in Ministry of Finance, Tax Bureau, *An Outline of Japanese Taxes*, where the only tax credits available to business are for purchases of certain types of energy-saving machinery.

Finally, a 20 percent income tax rate is assumed. Also, since capital gains are not taxed in Japan, the expression for the appropriate tax rate, θ, becomes $\theta = 0.2$ [dividends/ (dividends + retained earnings)].

61. Monthly stock prices for each firm and the Tokyo Stock Exchange index were obtained from *Japan Economic Journal*, various issues. Since Honda's stock was not publicly traded until 1972, it was not possible to estimate betas for this firm until 1976.

The formula used to calculate asset betas is $P_{i,t} = \alpha + \beta P_{mkt,t}$, where $P_{i,t}$ is the stock price of firm i at time t, and $P_{mkt,t}$ is the average stock price at time t.

These betas were then used to calculate the cost of equity. Other data necessary for this calculation were a risk premium and a risk-free rate of return. The risk-free rate of return is defined as the sixty-day treasury bill rate.[62] The risk premium is defined as the difference between some average stock market return and the risk-free rate.[63]

MATERIALS. The same methods used to derive material prices for the U.S. automakers were also used for the Japanese firms. The variable for the cost of materials was available in *Japan Economic Journal* data. To obtain the output of each manufacturer in pounds, figures for number of vehicles in each class were multiplied by the average weight of vehicles in that class, and then added together.[64]

OUTPUT. Annual production data for each Japanese firm were obtained from the Japanese Ministry of International Trade and Industry, aggregated into five output classes: minicars and trucks, compact cars and trucks, standard cars, standard trucks, and buses and motorcycles. The characteristics of the autos and trucks are given below.[65]

It was therefore assumed that the riskiness of Honda's stock between 1970 and 1975 could be represented by the average beta for the 1976–82 period.

62. This was obtained from Citibank's *World Financial Markets* for 1970–82.

63. The average return on stocks listed in the Tokyo Stock Exchange was calculated using the technique described in Ibbotson and Sinquefield, *Stocks*, p. 8. The market return is defined as $RM_t = (PM_t + DIV_t)/PM_{t-1}$, where RM_t is the average market return, PM_t is the arithmetic market average price for stocks on the Tokyo exchange from *Japan Statistical Yearbook*, and DIV_t is the average dividends paid, calculated using the average dividend rate listed in *Japan Statistical Yearbook*.

The resulting cost of equity was then combined with the cost of borrowing to yield a weighted average cost of capital, $\bar{r}$. The book value of bonds for each firm was taken from *Japan Economic Journal* data; the market value of equity was calculated using the number of outstanding shares of stock (from *Japan Economic Journal*) times the average stock price for each firm that year. A 40 percent corporate income tax was assumed. Finally, the cost of borrowing was represented by domestic corporate bond yields listed in *Japan Statistical Yearbook*.

Capital costs are defined as the sum of reported depreciation, interest expense, and dividend payments, since firm-specific data for these variables were available in *Japan Economic Journal*.

64. The specific weights were calculated using the specifications for vehicles produced in 1982 provided in *Automotive Herald's Guide to the Motor Industry of Japan, 1982* (Tokyo, 1982). A simple average weight for all vehicles within each class was computed for automobiles and trucks, while the midpoint of the range of weights was used as the average weight of a bus.

65. The source of the production data is Ministry of International Trade and Industry, *Yearbook of Machinery Statistics* (Tokyo, various issues, 1970–82).

	Width (m)	Length (m)	Piston displacement (cc)
Mini	<1.4	<3.2	<550
Compact	1.4–1.7	3.2–4.7	550–2,000
Standard	>1.7	>4.7	>2,000

INSTRUMENTS. The variables used as instruments for the output variables and sources were installment credit, unemployment rate, gas price, GNP, disposable income in constant yen, population, and consumption per capita. Data were obtained from the Japanese Bureau of Statistics, *Japan Statistical Yearbook*, various issues. The prime rate was obtained from Citibank's *World Financial Markets*, various issues, 1970-82. The market share for each firm and its absolute level of the particular output in the previous year were calculated using sales data provided in *Japan Economic Journal*.

DEFLATORS. All nominal data were deflated to 1975 dollars. Both the Japanese and U.S. data were deflated using the wholesale prices index given in International Monetary Fund, *International Financial Statistics*, various issues.

Table 2-9 gives the means and standard deviations of the U.S. and Japanese variables used in the cost functions.

Table 2-9. Descriptive Statistics of Variables Used in U.S. and Japan Automobile Cost Function Estimations

Variables	Description	Japan		United States	
		Mean	*Standard Deviation*	*Mean*	*Standard Deviation*
Outputs					
Y_c	Motorcycles	387,450	768,515	. . .	. . .
Y_m	Minicars	103,857	114,344	. . .	. . .
Y_s	Small cars	729,553	873,388	404,189	378,262
Y_l	Large cars	34,023	74,003	1,991,277	1,352,921
Y_t	Trucks, buses	50,917	79,656	584,328	369,947
Other variables					
W_k	Capital price	46.85[a]	14.04	34.54[a]	14.53
W_l	Wages	2,731.88[b]	660.28	18.13[c]	3.04
W_m	Materials price	188.49[b]	47.54	0.67[c]	0.17
C	Total costs	611,586,481[b]	574,611,847	17,000,799[c]	10,147,955

Source: Authors' data base.
a. Capital price is a price index.
b. Japanese wages per worker and total costs are given in thousands of 1975 yen; materials price is given in 1975 yen per pound of materials.
c. U.S. wages per worker and total costs are given in thousands of 1975 dollars; materials price is given in 1975 dollars per pound of materials.

CHAPTER THREE

U.S. Automobile Market Demand

FRED MANNERING and CLIFFORD WINSTON

DURING THE LATE 1980s the U.S. auto industry can expect to face its fiercest challenge ever from the Japanese industry. Japanese firms have already begun to establish substantial production capacity in the United States, and if the voluntary restraint agreement is not renewed after March 31, 1988, they will be allowed to export vehicles freely into the U.S. market.

U.S. auto industry sales, however, depend not just on actions by the Japanese industry but on the U.S. macroeconomy, exchange rates, and energy prices. In this chapter we forecast how U.S. automobile sales will fare for the remainder of this decade under alternative scenarios reflecting different levels of Japanese competition, constraints on international trade, and various macroeconomic conditions.

The Demand Forecasting System

Central to our forecasting system, diagramed in figure 3-1, are vehicle demand and vehicle scrappage models and an equilibrium model that determines market clearing prices of all new and used vehicles.

Into the models we put data on household characteristics, such as income; vehicle ownership experiences; characteristics of vehicles, such as prices; the stock of used vehicles; and sales restrictions on imported Japanese cars. We generated a pooled sample of vehicle purchasing behavior during 1978–80. The sample was updated to 1981–85 with actual

Figure 3-1. Vehicle Demand Forecasting System

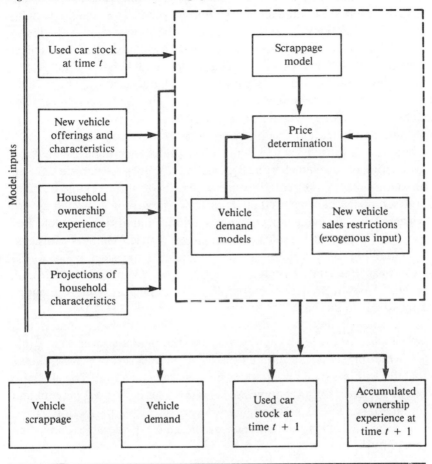

data and projected to 1990 with forecast data, including exogenous
forecasts of household characteristics, characteristics and prices of new
vehicles, and macroeconomic conditions.[1]

1. The data on household characteristics and ownership experiences are from the
Department of Energy's National Interim Energy Consumption Survey and the National
Transportation Panel. Vehicle characteristics were constructed from a vehicle attribute
file, and the stock of used vehicles from R. L. Polk Inc. For a detailed discussion of
the sample see Fred Mannering and Clifford Winston, "A Dynamic Empirical Analysis
of Household Vehicle Ownership and Utilization," *Rand Journal of Economics*, vol.
16 (Summer 1985), pp. 215–36.
    New model offerings are compiled in James Mateja, "Before Buying a New Car

The data are integrated with vehicle demand and vehicle scrappage models described in appendix A to this chapter.[2] The vehicle demand model characterizes households' choices about how many vehicles to own, what make, model, and vintage, and how many miles a vehicle is driven annually—choices depending on household characteristics, vehicle ownership experiences, and vehicle characteristics. The vehicle scrappage model characterizes the choice of whether to scrap a vehicle, a choice influenced by vehicle characteristics.

Automobile market equilibrium prices for new and used cars exist when new and used vehicle demand and vehicle scrappage equal the production of new vehicles and the existing stock of used vehicles. Given an automobile market equilibrium, current and future vehicle demand and scrappage can be predicted under various scenarios, which are triggered by changing specific parts of the equilibrium model. For example, U.S. industry sales without import restrictions can be forecast by removing the restriction in the model that the sales of Japanese exports in the United States cannot exceed 2.3 million vehicles. A technical description of the complete forecasting system is given in appendix A to this chapter.

The sales predictions of the equilibrium model can be compared with actual sales to evaluate the reliability of the model's forecasts. Table 3-1, which presents sales predictions by vehicle make for 1981–84, shows that the within-sample predictions are generally accurate. The absolute prediction error for total domestic sales is 0.1 percent to 5.1 percent and for total Japanese sales 0 percent to 2.6 percent. These prediction errors, which are small by previous standards, indicate considerable forecasting reliability.[3]

This Year Consider the Changes for 1986," *Philadelphia Inquirer*, February 17, 1985. Because data on new vehicle offerings do not include vehicles manufactured by Yugoslavian or Korean automakers, our forecasts do not account for the effect of these new competitors, although we do provide a qualitative assessment of their impact. They are also discussed in chapter 7.

The forecasts of household characteristics and macroeconomic conditions are based on the Wharton 20-year extension model published in Wharton Econometric Forecasting Associates, *Long-Term Alternative Scenarios and 20-Year Extension*, vol. 3, no. 4 (Philadelphia: Wharton, August 1985), app. A.

2. Both models were estimated with data from the late 1970s and early 1980s.

3. Using a similar approach, James Berkovec's model generated prediction errors for the same time period that were significantly higher than those obtained here. See "Forecasting Automobile Demand Using Disaggregate Choice Models," *Transportation Research*, vol. 19B (August 1985), pp. 315–29.

Demand Forecasts

By constructing a base case scenario and analyzing the impacts of deviations from it, we produce forecasts of U.S. automobile sales that consider the effects of intensified Japanese competition, changing import restrictions, varying exchange rates, and alternative macroeconomic environments.

The base case requires assumptions about the macroeconomy, parameters affecting international trade, and consumers' attitudes toward different makes of automobiles. From a number of different assumptions about real income growth and fuel prices, shown in table 3-2, we selected optimistic predictions of real income growth and of energy prices.[4] The assumptions we made for conditions affecting international trade are an exchange rate of 200 yen to the dollar and an absence of import restrictions.[5] The macroeconomic projections and the exchange rate are incorporated into the forecasting system by the demand model, which contains household income, fuel prices, and vehicle prices as explanatory variables.

A final assumption concerns consumer attitudes toward different vehicle makes. The demand model distinguishes between the effects of brand preference and brand loyalty. Brand preference is defined as the consumer's tendency to purchase a specific make of car and is largely influenced by the extent of the make's dealer network, repair service, parts availability, and the consumer's nationalistic preferences toward American or foreign cars.[6] Our estimation results indicate that Ford and General Motors have the greatest potential to benefit from brand preference. We assume for the base case that brand preferences are un-

4. Without import restrictions, the new car prices that correspond to Wharton's optimistic real income scenario grow slightly faster than the rate of inflation: 1.00 in 1985, 1.03 in 1987, 1.04 in 1988, 1.06 in 1989, and 1.07 in 1990. See *Long-Term Alternative Scenarios*. Japanese new car prices are assumed to rise at the same rate as inflation. U.S. and Japanese new car prices are determined endogenously by the forecasting system when import restrictions are in effect.

5. The assumption about the exchange rate is a compromise based on recent historical levels. We also provide forecasts that capture the significant appreciation of the yen that occurred during 1985–86 and forecasts that reflect the level of exchange rates before this appreciation.

6. The extent of brand preference is shown by indicators of vehicle make in tables 3-7 and 3-8, appendix B to this chapter. These indicators also capture additional effects pertaining to a vehicle make that are less important than those noted above.

Table 3-1. Actual and Predicted Automobile Sales in the United States, 1981–84

Automobile make	1981			1982		
	Actual	Predicted	Percent difference	Actual	Predicted	Percent difference
American Motors	136,682	135,308	-1.0	82,260	63,877	-22.3
Renault	0	0	0	30,173	35,466	17.5
Total American Motors	136,682	135,308	-1.0	112,433	99,343	-11.6
Buick	722,617	703,420	-2.6	723,011	707,209	-2.2
Cadillac	230,665	263,904	14.4	249,295	267,317	7.2
Chevrolet	1,442,218	1,402,098	-2.8	1,260,620	1,317,018	4.5
Oldsmobile	848,739	813,873	-4.1	799,585	786,285	-1.7
Pontiac	552,394	512,979	-7.1	483,149	483,827	0.0
Total General Motors	3,796,696	3,696,274	-2.6	3,515,660	3,561,656	1.3
Ford	977,220	966,815	-1.1	925,490	949,944	2.6
Mercury	339,550	341,471	0.1	327,142	335,090	2.4
Lincoln	63,830	70,996	11.2	93,068	75,977	-18.4
Total Ford	1,380,600	1,379,282	0.0	1,345,700	1,361,011	1.1
Chrysler	93,869	103,506	10.3	176,369	120,536	-24.0
Dodge	305,757	299,413	-2.1	261,105	289,900	11.0
Plymouth	325,598	340,030	4.4	251,628	310,882	23.8
Total Chrysler	725,224	742,949	2.4	689,102	721,318	4.7
Total Domestic	6,206,296	6,016,327	-3.1	5,756,660	5,803,632	0.1
Nissan	464,805	474,047	2.0	470,246	482,016	2.5
Honda	370,705	353,705	-4.6	365,865	352,908	-3.5
Mazda	166,088	154,280	-7.1	163,150	158,008	-3.1
Subaru	152,062	153,519	0.1	150,335	150,645	0.0
Toyota	576,491	544,759	-5.5	530,246	521,585	-1.6
Mitsubishi	110,940	125,133	12.8	106,227	118,494	11.5
Total Japanese	1,858,091	1,865,143	0.1	1,801,481	1,848,329	2.6
Total U.S. Sales	8,531,514	8,292,101	-2.8	7,977,570	8,051,600	0.1

| | 1983 | | | 1984 | | |
Automobile make	Actual	Predicted	Percent difference	Actual	Predicted	Percent difference
American Motors	47,161	38,343	−18.7	20,654	35,923	74.0
Renault	146,190	159,884	9.4	169,601	176,680	4.2
Total American Motors	193,351	198,227	2.5	190,255	212,603	11.7
Buick	845,083	812,922	−3.8	941,611	911,672	−3.2
Cadillac	300,337	310,490	3.4	320,017	358,298	11.9
Chevrolet	1,347,447	1,425,734	5.8	1,565,143	1,573,911	0.1
Oldsmobile	1,007,559	928,648	−7.8	1,056,053	973,332	−7.8
Pontiac	553,135	536,579	−3.0	704,684	647,212	−8.2
Total General Motors	4,053,561	4,014,373	0.1	4,587,508	4,464,425	−2.7
Ford	1,060,314	1,055,114	0.0	1,300,644	1,244,428	−4.3
Mercury	409,433	374,271	−8.6	527,198	485,275	−8.0
Lincoln	101,574	107,740	6.1	151,475	133,814	−11.7
Total Ford	1,571,321	1,537,125	−2.2	1,979,317	1,863,517	−5.9
Chrysler	260,861	232,065	−11.0	328,499	257,743	−21.5
Dodge	313,977	338,192	7.7	369,255	342,331	−7.3
Plymouth	265,608	314,148	18.3	289,244	329,118	13.8
Total Chrysler	840,446	884,405	5.2	986,998	929,192	−5.9
Total Domestic	6,795,302	6,703,788	−1.4	7,951,517	7,548,168	−5.1
Nissan	521,902	479,307	−8.2	485,298	473,046	−2.5
Honda	350,670	371,838	6.0	374,819	370,978	−1.0
Mazda	173,388	167,753	−3.2	169,666	167,507	−1.3
Subaru	156,840	157,047	0.0	157,385	155,048	−1.5
Toyota	555,766	556,432	0.0	557,981	556,169	0.0
Mitsubishi	136,324	150,513	5.5	130,822	185,314	41.6
Total Japanese	1,915,621	1,922,937	0.0	1,906,208	1,912,249	0.0
Total U.S. Sales	9,181,366	9,057,241	−1.4	10,393,230	9,925,388	−4.5

Sources: *Automotive News*, various issues 1981–84; and authors' calculations.

Table 3-2. Projections of U.S. Real Income Growth and Fuel Prices, 1987–90

Scenario	1987	1988	1989	1990
Real income growth[a]				
Optimistic[b]	1.062	1.089	1.124	1.142
Pessimistic[c]	1.027	1.053	1.071	1.080
Very pessimistic[d]	0.945	0.923	0.905	0.887
Fuel prices[e]				
Very optimistic	0.85	0.85	0.85	0.85
Optimistic[b]	1.09	1.10	1.11	1.10
Pessimistic[c]	1.11	1.12	1.12	1.12
Disaster[f]	2.22	2.44	2.69	2.95

Sources: Wharton Econometric Forecasting Associates, *Long-Term Alternative Scenarios and 20-Year Extension,* vol. 3, no. 4 (Philadelphia: Wharton, August 1985). (Hereafter, Wharton 20-year extension model.)
 a. 1985 = 1.00.
 b. See 1985 Wharton 20-year extension model, pp. A-9, A-39.
 c. See 1985 Wharton lower growth alternative model, pp. C-9, C-39.
 d. Pessimistic scenario but with 8 percent decline in income in 1987 and 2 percent decline each year thereafter.
 e. Constant 1985 dollars a gallon.
 f. Fuel prices double in 1987 and increase 10 percent a year thereafter.

changed from the demand estimation results. The process through which brand loyalty is developed consists of the accumulation of information, through driving and ownership experience, on particular vehicle makes.[7] Estimation of the demand model revealed very strong effects of brand loyalty for all makes.[8] We assume these effects do not change during the forecast period. The development of brand loyalty for foreign makes and the maintenance of brand loyalty for U.S. makes induces some sluggishness in consumers' responses to our projected changes in the automobile market. Brand loyalty toward foreign makes causes difficulties for domestic firms trying to recapture lost market shares; brand loyalty toward domestic makes limits the degree of import penetration, at least in the short run.

Results

We first assume intensified competition as a result of higher Japanese automobile production in America that increases brand preference for Japanese makes. The justification for this assumption is based on Mannering and Chu Te's empirical analysis of the effect of where vehicles

7. Brand loyalty is captured by lagged utilization variables. The coefficients for these variables were highly significant (see tables 3-7 and 3-8, appendix B to this chapter).

8. Lagged utilization variables were not specified by manufacturer because this would unrealistically imply that learning processes differ according to vehicle make.

are manufactured on vehicle demand.[9] They found that households exhibiting strong preferences favored vehicles manufactured in the United States regardless of brand. A preference for American-made, foreign-brand vehicles reflects such factors favoring foreign brands as corporate quality control and such factors favoring vehicles made in America as parts and repair availability and national pride.[10] Table 3-3 presents 1990 demand forecasts for the base case and for two cases of increased preference for Japanese makes. Without such increased preference, the U.S. industry will experience reasonably healthy sales— roughly 8 million vehicles—despite the absence of restrictions on Japanese sales. In this case the market share of Japanese firms is close to what it was before the quotas were imposed in 1981. An increase in brand preference for Japanese makes, however, would pose a serious threat to U.S. industry sales and allow the Japanese automakers' share to exceed 40 percent as they cut into sales of new U.S. vehicles and attract buyers from used car markets. Although sales of new U.S. vehicles would fall by nearly 10 percent, brand loyalty would prevent a precipitous decline in sales.

Import Restrictions and Exchange Rates

U.S. government policies that affect international trade are also a major influence on the demand for American cars. According to demand forecasts that assume current import restrictions of 2.3 million vehicles, shown in table 3-3, the Japanese market share would fall almost 4 percentage points from what it would be in an unrestricted environment. To forecast how these restrictions will affect U.S. new car sales, we incorporated U.S. manufacturers' responses to Japanese price increases resulting from the restrictions and find that U.S. new car sales are actually lower under the restrictions.[11] This occurs because U.S. firms

9. Fred L. Mannering and Grace O. Chu Te, "Evidence on the Impacts of Manufacturer Sourcing on Vehicle Demand," *Transportation Research Record*, forthcoming.

10. An evaluation of the Toyota Corolla that is made by American workers under Toyota management (as part of the General Motors–Toyota joint venture) describes the vehicle as having "world-class craftsmanship." See Warren Brown, "Corolla FX-16: Small Box, Big Ticket," *Washington Post*, November 29, 1986.

11. This response is called the conjectural elasticity of U.S. prices with respect to Japanese prices. Robert W. Crandall estimates this elasticity to be 0.4. Thus a 10 percent increase in Japanese auto prices leads U.S. producers to raise their prices by 4 percent.

Table 3-3. U.S. Automobile Demand in 1990 under Intensified Japanese Competition, Import Restrictions, or Varying Exchange Rates

Thousands of vehicles unless otherwise indicated

Scenario	American Motors	General Motors	Ford	Chrysler	Total domestic[a]	Total Japanese	Percent Japanese	Total imports	Total sales[a]
Base case									
Optimistic economy and energy prices, no import restrictions, brand preferences unchanged, exchange rate 200 yen/dollar	285.3	4,498.8	2,045.8	913.5	7,846.1	2,984.3	26.5	3,407.8	11,253.9
Intensified Japanese competition									
Preference for Japanese brands equal to that for General Motors	278.0	4,238.7	1,905.3	880.1	7,389.3	5,401.7	41.0	5,819.0	13,208.8
Preference for Japanese brands higher than that for any U.S. manufacturer	274.8	4,130.5	1,847.1	866.8	7,200.8	6,293.4	45.3	6,706.7	13,907.5
Import restrictions									
Japanese imports restricted to 2.3 million vehicles; Japanese new car prices set to meet restrictions[b]	273.4	4,244.2	1,920.4	878.5	7,409.5	2,308.7	22.8	2,711.5	10,121.0
Japanese imports restricted to 2.3 million vehicles; Japanese new car prices set to meet restrictions; preference for Japanese brands equal to that for General Motors by 1990[c]	266.9	4,022.2	1,800.5	849.4	7,019.5	3,862.2	34.2	4,259.5	11,279.1
Varying exchange rates									
Exchange rate 150 yen/dollar	287.5	4,533.9	2,062.2	919.7	7,906.7	2,587.3	23.7	3,013.3	10,920.0
Exchange rate 250 yen/dollar	283.7	4,464.1	2,027.9	909.0	7,785.9	3,509.1	30.0	3,929.5	11,715.4

Source: Authors' calculations.

a. Totals may not add because of rounding.

b. Assumes a conjectural elasticity of 0.4.

c. Assumes a conjectural elasticity of 0.4. Also assumes Japanese firms attempt to avoid quotas by increasing by 10 percent a year in 1987–90 the number of vehicles they sell in the U.S. market that are made in U.S.-based plants. Prices for these vehicles would still be sensitive to the existing restrictions (a Toyota Camry made in the United States, for instance, would sell for the same price as one made in Japan).

increase their prices in response to the Japanese quota-induced price increases to the point that, although they generate lower sales than in an unrestricted environment, they increase profits.[12]

An increase in U.S.-based production of Japanese autos in response to the quotas, thus increasing Japanese brand preference, increases the Japanese market share significantly, while U.S. firms' sales fall by 5 percent, even with import sales restrictions in effect. In this respect trade restrictions actually hurt the U.S. automobile industry by encouraging foreign firms to increase U.S.-based production that can erode brand preference.[13]

Exchange rate fluctuations have a noticeable effect on Japanese sales and used car sales (table 3-3).[14] Thus government policy that contributes to lower dollar exchange rates will reduce the Japanese market share and improve the trade balance. Indeed, we forecast that the appreciation of the yen during 1985–86 would reduce the Japanese market share by at least 5 percentage points if this reduction were immediately reflected in relative prices. Any fall in Japanese sales caused by lower exchange rates that increase Japanese vehicle prices would not necessarily gen-

---

See "Assessing the Impacts of the Automobile Voluntary Export Restraints Upon U.S. Automobile Prices," paper delivered to the Society of Government Economists, New York, December 1985.

12. The impact of import restrictions on automobile firms' profitability is discussed fully in chapter 4.

13. To be sure, the dramatic appreciation of the yen in 1985–86 may have ultimately influenced Japanese companies to develop automobile manufacturing capacity in the United States. As recently as August 1986, however, Toyota indicated it would increase emphasis on North American manufacturing because of concerns about tightened quotas on Japanese car exports to the United States. See "Toyota to Stress U.S. Production," *New York Times*, August 11, 1986.

Japanese firms that increase their U.S.-based production have an ambiguous effect on U.S. automobile employment and the trade balance. By hiring American workers, Japanese firms increase U.S. automobile employment, but by eroding brand preference toward American makes, thus reducing American manufacturers' sales, they reduce the U.S. manufacturers' domestic work force. By producing vehicles in the United States, Japanese firms increase the American value added in the production of their vehicles, thus reducing the U.S. trade deficit with Japan. However, to the extent that the increase in American value added occurs at the expense of U.S. manufactuers' sales, the reduction in the trade balance is offset.

14. These forecasts assume changes in exchange rates are automatically reflected in new vehicle prices. Consistent with recent behavior by most domestic automakers, we do not assume that domestic new car prices change in response to exchange rate fluctuations. Allowing them to do so would lessen the sales response forecast here.

Table 3-4. U.S. Automobile Demand in 1990 under Alternative Macroeconomic Environments

Thousands of vehicles unless otherwise specified

Scenario	American Motors	General Motors	Ford	Chrysler	Total domestic[a]	Total Japanese	Percent Japanese	Total imports	Total sales[a]
Base case									
Optimistic economy and energy prices, no import restrictions, brand preferences unchanged, exchange rate of 200 yen/dollar	285.3	4,498.8	2,045.8	913.5	7,846.1	2,984.3	26.5	3,407.8	11,253.9
Alternative environments									
Very optimistic energy prices from 1987 on ($0.85 a gallon)	300.0	4,809.0	2,204.2	955.0	8,382.7	2,978.7	25.2	3,429.6	11,812.3
Very optimistic energy prices from 1987 on ($0.85 a gallon) and preference for Japanese brands equal to that for General Motors	281.8	4,325.3	1,953.5	891.3	7,543.4	5,207.9	39.5	5,633.6	13,177.0
Pessimistic economy and pessimistic energy prices ($1.12 a gallon)	271.7	4,213.0	1,904.4	874.2	7,355.4	2,927.1	27.4	3,326.7	10,682.1
Very pessimistic economy, disastrous energy prices ($2.95 a gallon) and preference for Japanese brands equal to that for General Motors	195.0	2,639.1	1,114.5	640.0	4,622.1	4,157.3	45.9	4,431.2	9,053.3

Source: Authors' calculations.
a. Totals may not add because of rounding.

erate much greater sales of new American cars because the relative attractiveness of used cars would increase significantly.[15]

Alternative Macroeconomic Environments

The recent fall in energy prices has generally benefited the U.S. economy and will especially improve the fortunes of U.S. manufacturers (table 3-4). Consumers will increase their purchases of less fuel efficient cars, which favors U.S. producers. If brand preference toward Japanese automakers improves, this response will be offset and Japanese sales will increase. A weaker economy and a rise in energy prices would lead to a sizable drop in U.S. sales. The combination of a very weak economy, very high energy prices, and a change in brand preferences—that is, an environment similar to 1979 automobile market conditions—would be calamitous for U.S. automakers. U.S. industry sales would fall below 5 million vehicles, approaching the lowest sales figures of the past thirty-five years, and the Japanese market share would reach nearly 50 percent.

Implications of Demand Forecasts

For all but the worst energy and macroeconomic scenarios, the demand forecasts indicate that U.S. industry sales will be reasonably strong—at least 7.5 million vehicles annually—for the remainder of the decade, even without quotas. By way of comparison, U.S. new car sales in 1985 (when restrictions were in effect) were slightly greater than 8.0 million vehicles. Given current technology and recent industry cost reductions, the forecast level of sales should be profitable.[16] At least it was in 1974–75 when between 7.0 and 7.5 million new U.S. cars were sold each year, and annual industry profits were roughly $1 billion.

A major but unlikely threat to industry profitability is a return to 1979 automobile market conditions.[17] A more genuine threat is a significant

15. As indicated in chapter 2, however, changes in exchange rates have significant implications for cost competitiveness.

16. U.S. automobile employment will still fall at this level of sales because of the industry's greater use of modular assembly and its development of less labor-intensive plants, such as the General Motors Saturn plant in Tennessee.

17. In the final months of 1985, crude oil prices fell by one-third, to less than $20 a barrel. Current prices are half what they were at their peak in 1981 and are not expected to rise significantly in the near future.

increase in brand preference for Japanese makes. The U.S. industry is attempting to respond to this challenge by developing American nameplate vehicles manufactured by foreign automakers, thus offering consumers the vehicle quality associated with foreign producers combined with American firms' vast service networks.[18] It is unclear, however, whether in the long run this strategy will strengthen brand preference toward American franchises or toward vehicles manufactured by foreign firms.

As already noted, government policy is partly responsible for the challenge to brand preference for American cars. The imposition of quotas in 1981 encouraged Japanese firms to make such strategic shifts as upgrading product quality and moving plants to the United States.[19] If the advantage in brand preference held by U.S. automakers is significantly eroded by foreign firms that engage in substantial U.S.-based production, as we expect, then the long-run impact of the quotas on the U.S. automobile industry will not serve the interests of the protected industry.[20]

Government policy can best help the U.S. automobile industry by contributing to a stable economic environment that does not present opportunities for established foreign firms to erode brand preference for U.S. makes or provide new foreign entrants with significant opportunities to develop brand loyalty.[21] Policies that contribute to reductions in dollar exchange rates and to lower energy prices will lessen the trade deficit by reducing Japanese new car sales, but they will not provide a huge boost to sales of new American vehicles. This can only be accomplished by the U.S. companies.[22]

---

18. The domestic models most successful in recapturing market shares from imports are American nameplate vehicles built by foreign automakers. See *Power Report* (May 1986), p. 5.

19. José A. Gomez-Ibañez, Robert A. Leone, and Stephen A. O'Connell, "Restraining Auto Imports: Does Anyone Win?" *Journal of Policy Analysis and Management,* vol. 2, no. 2 (1983), pp. 196–219.

20. Chapter 4 presents a complete analysis of the economic effects of automobile quotas.

21. For example, the new Korean and Yugoslavian producers of low-cost, fuel-efficient vehicles would find it easier to penetrate the U.S. market and to develop brand loyalty toward their cars in an economy characterized by high energy prices and high inflation. In addition, U.S. producers appear ready to compete with the new entrants. Ford and General Motors have lined up foreign sources for low-priced small cars, and Chrysler is offering a low-priced version of the Dodge Omni/Plymouth Horizon.

22. One potentially effective strategy for increasing industry sales may be the low-

Appendix A: Technical Description of Demand Forecasting System

The demand forecasting system incorporates disaggregate automobile demand and usage models in a model of market equilibrium. The disaggregate demand models are the basis for an aggregate demand function used to forecast vehicle demand. The equilibrium model is based on and extends the model of James Berkovec[23] by solving for the complete price vector of every vehicle make, model, and vintage from the 1969 model year onward and by using a demand system that accounts for dynamic considerations (previous vehicle ownership, for instance) and the interrelated choices of vehicle quantity, type, and use.

Model Structure

Market equilibrium requires that the production of new U.S. and foreign vehicles and the existing stock of used vehicles equal consumer demand for new and used vehicles and the number of vehicles scrapped. This relationship at time t is specified as

$$(3\text{-}1) \qquad Q^t(P^t, X^t) + J^t(P^t, X^t) + I^t(P^t, X^t) + S^t$$
$$= R^t(P^t, X^t) + D^t(P^t, X^t, Z^t, Y^t),$$

where Q^t is the production of new domestic vehicles available for the U.S. market, P^t is the matrix of vehicle prices, X^t is the matrix of vehicle characteristics, J^t is the production of new Japanese vehicles available for the U.S. market, I^t is the production of new non-Japanese imports available for the U.S. market, S^t is the existing stock of used vehicles, R^t is the number of vehicles scrapped, D^t is the consumer demand for new and used vehicles, Z^t is the matrix of consumer characteristics, and Y^t is the matrix of consumer vehicle experiences. Note that Q^t, J^t, I^t, and

---

cost vehicle financing programs that have gained widespread use by the industry. These programs particularly appear to help the relative sales of less technologically advanced vehicles. See Fred L. Mannering. "Analysis of the Impact of Interest Rates on Automobile Demand," working paper (Pennsylvania State University, July 1986). Cut-rate financing programs have, however, been cited by General Motors as a main contributor to its 1986 third-quarter operating loss.

23. "Forecasting Automobile Demand"; see also Berkovec, "New Car Sales and Used Car Stocks: A Model of the Automobile Market," *Rand Journal of Economics*, vol. 16 (Summer 1985), pp. 195–214.

R^t are functions of the prices and characteristics of available vehicles, while D^t is a function of vehicle prices and characteristics and consumer characteristics and experiences with vehicles. Because S^t represents the available stock of used vehicles it is exogenously given. In addition to the equilibrium condition, we have the identity that today's consumer demand, D^t, must equal tomorrow's used vehicle stock, S^{t+1}:

$$(3\text{-}2) \qquad\qquad S^{t+1} = Q^t(P^t, X^t, Z^t, Y^t).$$

We now describe the elements of equation 3-1 in detail.

Production of New Vehicles

A firm's production of various models and its pricing strategies depend on a variety of factors, including input costs, competition, and so on. Developing models to forecast these industrial decisions is beyond the scope of this work. Instead, we make some basic assumptions regarding the production and pricing of new vehicles that are historically consistent with automakers' behavior.

In the absence of sales restrictions (import restrictions, for example), manufacturers will set prices at the beginning of each year and let vehicles clear the market at those prices. The assumption of perfectly elastic supply is not unrealistic because most vehicle models are assembled at production levels that are well below plant capacity. Thus capacity constraints are not likely to be encountered. We also assume that vehicle characteristics are not endogenously determined.

Manufacturers' model offerings (and their associated characteristics) and vehicles planned for production are assumed to be insensitive to changes in vehicle demand. This assumption is reasonable given the usual four to five years between vehicle design and actual production. Expected model offerings by manufacturers to 1990 are obtained from various sources.[24]

If sales restrictions are imposed on new vehicles, their prices will rise until a market clearing price is achieved. For example, suppose Japanese manufacturers price their vehicles at P_j and the disaggregate demand models predict Q_j Japanese vehicles will be sold. If import restrictions constrain sales to some lower level, then prices will rise above P_j to

24. These are compiled in James Mateja, "Before Buying a New Car This Year Consider the Changes for 1986," *Philadelphia Inquirer*, February 17, 1985.

ensure the sales restriction is met. Prices for domestic new cars will also rise in accordance with U.S. automakers' conjectural elasticity.

Vehicle Scrappage

Vehicle scrappage is a function of vehicle characteristics and prices. The scrappage model developed by Berkovec is used here.[25] The model assumes the following functional form:

$$(3\text{-}3) \qquad \phi_i = \exp\left[\beta_0 + X_i\,\beta + \gamma\,P_i + \alpha\,P_i^2 + u_i\right],$$

where ϕ_i is the probability of scrappage for vehicle type i, P_i is the price of vehicle type i, X_i is the vector of characteristics of vehicle type i, u_i is the error term, and β_0, β, γ, and α are parameters.

The expected scrappage for any vehicle type i is thus

$$(3\text{-}4) \qquad R_i^t\,(P_i^t, X_i^t) = \phi_i\,(X_i^t, P_i^t)\,S_i^t,$$

where S_i^t is the quantity of vehicles of type i in existence at the beginning of time period t.

Berkovec estimated the parameters of equation 3-3 using data from 1978 scrappage rates. The results of this estimation, which are used in the equilibrium model, are presented in table 3-5 in appendix B.

Vehicle Demand

The demand system used here was developed previously by the authors.[26] This system gives explicit consideration of households' inter-related choices of how many vehicles to own, what types, and the extent to which a vehicle is used. The dynamic aspects of vehicle ownership are accounted for by lagged utilization variables that capture taste changes and previous ownership experience.

The derivation of the demand system is as follows. The stochastic dynamic utilization equation for a given household is specified in a linear form as

$$(3\text{-}5) \qquad \begin{aligned} X_{it} = {} & A_{i0} + A_{i1}\,X_{it-1} + A_{i2}X_{it-2} + A_{i3}\,X'_{it-1} \\ & + A_{i4}X'_{it-2} + Z'_{it}\,\theta + v_t, \end{aligned}$$

25. Berkovec, "New Car Sales and Used Car Stocks."

26. Fred Mannering and Clifford Winston, "A Dynamic Empirical Analysis of Household Vehicle Ownership and Utilization," *Rand Journal of Economics*, vol. 16 (Summer 1985), pp. 215–36.

where (using discrete time) X_{it} is the accumulated utilization of vehicle i over the discrete time interval, X_{it-1} and X_{it-2} are the utilization of vehicle i lagged by one and two periods respectively, X'_{it-1} and X'_{it-2} are the accumulated utilization over the discrete time interval of a vehicle (not including vehicle i) that is the same make as vehicle i lagged by one and two periods respectively, Z'_{it} is a vector of household and vehicle characteristics, the A_i's are parameters, θ is a parameter vector, and v_t is a disturbance term.

The indirect utility function that corresponds to this utilization equation can be derived by Roy's Identity,

$$(3\text{-}6) \qquad V_{it} = [A_{i0} - \Pi_i\, r_{it} + A_{i1}\, X_{it-1} + A_{i2}\, X_{it-2} + A_{i3}\, X'_{it-1}$$
$$+ A_{i4}\, X'_{it-2} + Z'_{it}\, \theta + v_t] e^{-A_{i5} P_{it}} + \epsilon_{it},$$

where r_{it} is the typical utilization (calculated from aggregate average utilizations) of vehicle i in period t, P_{it} is the unit price of vehicle utilization, Π is a parameter, and ϵ_{it} is an additional disturbance term.

Given this specification of utility, it can be shown that the probability of selecting vehicle type i conditional on n vehicles being selected, $P_{in|n}$, and the marginal probability of n vehicles being selected, P_n, is given by the nested multinomial logit form as

$$(3\text{-}7) \qquad\qquad P_{in|n} = \frac{e^{V_{in|n}}}{\sum\limits_{in} e^{V_{i'n|n}}},$$

$$(3\text{-}8) \qquad\qquad P_n = \frac{e^{[V_n + \zeta L_n]}}{\sum\limits_{n'} e^{[V_{n'} + \zeta L_{n'}]}},$$

$$(3\text{-}9) \qquad\qquad L_n = \log\left[\sum\limits_{in} \exp\left(\overline{V}_{in|n}\right)\right],$$

where $\overline{V}_{in|n}$ is the nonstochastic utility from vehicle type conditional on vehicle quantity, $\overline{V}_n$ is the nonstochastic utility from vehicle quantity, ζ is a parameter, and L_n is the inclusive value (also called the log sum) interpreted as the expected value of the maximum utility obtained from the choice over all vehicle types.[27] It reflects the importance of households' satisfaction in vehicle ownership in determining the number to own.

---

27. To be consistent with utility maximization, it is necessary for the log sum coefficient to have a value between zero and one.

The utilization (3-5), vehicle type (3-7), and vehicle quantity (3-8) equations were estimated with data from one- and two-vehicle households from 1978 to 1980.[28] Because only 7.8 percent of all households own three or more vehicles, our omission of these households from the demand estimation was not particularly important.[29] Estimation results and elasticities for these models for 1980 are given in tables 3-6 through 3-10 in appendix B.[30]

Based on this system, the demand for any vehicle type i is determined by

$$(3\text{-}10) \qquad D_i^t(P_i^t, X_i^t, Z^t, Y_i^t) = H\left[\sum_k \sum_n P_n^{k*} P_{i|n}^k\right],$$

where H is the ratio of the number of U.S. households to the number of sample households used for forecasting (726), k denotes a sample household, P_n^k is the marginal probability of n vehicles being selected, $P_{i|n}^k$ is the probability of selecting vehicle type i conditional on n vehicles being selected, and other notation is as defined previously. The utilization of all type i vehicles, U_i^t, is obtained from the demand models as

$$(3\text{-}11) \qquad U_i^t = H\left[\sum_k \sum_n P_n^{k*} U_{i|n}^k\right],$$

where $U_{i|n}$ is the utilization of vehicle i conditional on owning n vehicles.[31] Note that the U_i^t calculated in equation 3-11 becomes input into the type choice, quantity choice, and utilization equations in year $t + 1$. The number of future households and the matrix of future consumer characteristics is obtained from the demographic forecasts of the Wharton 20-year extension model.

28. For those households that choose to own two vehicles, the specification of the indirect utility function for the type-choice decision and the specification of the utilization equation refer to the combination of vehicles or total utilization that corresponds to a given vehicle portfolio.

29. As indicated by the estimation results in appendix B to this chapter, single-vehicle and two-vehicle households' preferences are similar. The preferences of households owning three or more vehicles are probably not much different from those of single- and two vehicle households. Our forecasts assume the shares of households with three or more vehicles and those with none remain unchanged from the base forecasting period.

30. The 1980 period reflects type choice as of January 1980 and utilization from January 1980 to June 1980.

31. The impact of vehicle type choice on vehicle utilization is accounted for by the instrumental variables procedure described in Mannering and Winston, "Household Vehicle Ownership."

Equilibrium Conditions

Equilibrium is determined at each target year when market clearing prices are obtained. An equilibrium can be defined for each used vehicle type i at time t as

(3-12) $S_i^t = D_i^t(P_i^t) + R_i^t(P_i^t)$,

where S_i^t is the supply of used vehicle type i, $D_i^t(P_i^t)$ is the demand for used vehicle type i at price P_i, and $R_i^t(P_i^t)$ is the scrappage demand for used vehicle type i at price P_i.

For new vehicles, because it is assumed that prices are fixed unless a sales restriction occurs, demand determines production: $D_{iD}(P,X,Z,Y)$ $\longrightarrow Q_i(P_i,X_i)$; $D_{iJ}(P,X,Z,Y) \longrightarrow J_i(P_i,X_i)$; and $D_{iI}(P,X,Z,Y) \longrightarrow I_i(P_i,X_i)$. D_{iD}, D_{iJ}, and D_{iI} are the demands for domestic, Japanese, and other imports at predetermined prices. If restrictions are imposed, prices are determined to ensure that the following equality is satisfied:

(3-13) $R_i = D_i(P,X,Z,Y)$,

where R_i is the restricted sales quantity for vehicle type i. Of course, this equality can be applied over a class of vehicle types such as all Japanese models. Given an automobile market equilibrium, forecasts of vehicle demand can be obtained for a variety of scenarios.

Appendix B: Estimation Results for Scrappage and Demand Models

Table 3-5. Scrappage Model Definitions and Estimation Results[a]

Variable	Description and example		Coefficient	T-statistic
Constant			-0.5906	-1.212
Price[b]			-2.218	-4.102
Price ** 2[b]			0.2630	3.923
D67[c]			-0.02039	-0.342
D68			-0.01180	-0.0282
D69			-0.0784	-0.1732
D70			-0.0448	-0.1146
D71			0.0820	0.2804
D72			0.0539	0.2610
D73			0.01667	0.1277
Class 1	Domestic subcompact	(Ford Pinto)	...	...
Class 2[d]	Domestic compact	(Dodge Dart)	-0.3778	-2.33
Class 3	Domestic sporty	(Chevrolet Camaro)	0.0455	0.265
Class 4	Domestic intermediate	(Chevrolet Malibu)	-0.3165	-1.824
Class 5	Domestic standard	(Chevrolet Impala)	-0.6745	-2.646
Class 6	Domestic luxury	(Cadillac)	-0.4180	-1.696
Class 7	Foreign subcompact	(Toyota Corolla)	-0.0935	-0.5190
Class 8	Foreign larger	(Volvo)	0.0277	0.1150
Class 9	Sports	(Porsche)	0.5480	1.390
Class 10	Foreign luxury	(Mercedes)	-0.3333	-0.7670
Class 11	Pickup truck		0.5574	1.799
Class 12	Van		0.5146	1.574
Class 13	Utility vehicle	(Jeep)	1.200	2.611
Weight[e]			0.0928	0.6688
Old truck[f]			-0.7750	-3.498

Number of observations, 531; standard error, .508; SSR, 131.
Exogeneity test values = 5.99 distributed as $\chi^2(2)$ (rejects hypothesis of exogenous prices at 5 percent level)

Source: James Berkovec, "Forecasting Automobile Demand Using Disaggregate Choice Models," *Transportation Research*, vol. 19B (August 1985), pp. 319–20.
a. Dependent variable is the probability of scrapping vehicle type i at time t (i denotes make, model, and vintage).
b. Thousands of 1978 dollars. Instrumental variables estimates for price terms.
c. Dummy variable for the 1967 model year.
d. Dummy variable for class 2, domestic compacts.
e. Vehicle curb weight.
f. Dummy variable if truck (classes 11, 12, and 13) is older than 7 years.

Table 3-6. Vehicle Type-Choice Elasticities for Single-Vehicle and Two-Vehicle Households[a]

	Single-vehicle household			Two-vehicle household		
Vehicle	Income	Capital costs	Operating costs	Income	Capital costs	Operating costs
Compact						
1972 Chevrolet Vega	0.881	−0.180	−0.647	0.994	−0.241	−0.806
1972 Toyota Corolla	0.968	−0.237	−0.726	1.03	−0.262	−0.816
1979 Chevrolet Chevette	1.58	−0.980	−0.598	1.22	−0.511	−0.758
1979 Toyota Corolla	1.67	−1.06	−0.595	1.25	−0.543	−0.755
Midsize						
1972 Ford Maverick	1.17	−0.253	−0.913	1.11	−0.266	−0.903
1979 Ford Granada	2.01	−1.09	−0.908	1.39	−0.548	−0.898
Full size						
1972 Oldsmobile Cutlass	1.57	−0.331	−1.23	1.28	−0.293	−1.04
1979 Oldsmobile Cutlass	2.05	−1.13	−0.908	1.41	−0.565	−0.894

Source: Authors' calculations.

a. Elasticities were calculated by using the formula $\partial P_{i_{n/n}} / \partial k \cdot k / P_{i_{n/n}}$ where $P_{i\,n/n}$ is the probability of choosing vehicle type i conditional on n vehicles being selected, and k is an explanatory variable. Estimates were obtained by enumerating through the household sample.

Table 3-7. Type-Choice Model Estimates for Single-Vehicle Households[a]

Explanatory variable	Coefficient[b]	Explanatory variable	Coefficient[b]
Annual fuel cost ÷ annual income (dollars)[c]	−31.41 (7.85)	American Motors indicator (1 if AMC; 0 otherwise)	−0.901 (0.487)
Vehicle capital cost ÷ annual income (dollars)[d]	−2.45 (0.522)	Ford indicator (1 if Ford; 0 otherwise)	0.298 (0.223)
One-period lagged utilization same vehicle (thousands of miles)	0.591 (0.0709)	Chrysler indicator (1 if Chrysler; 0 otherwise)	−0.799 (0.299)
Two-period lagged utilization same vehicle (thousands of miles)	0.414 (0.0745)	Foreign car indicator (1 if foreign car; 0 otherwise)	−1.36 (0.387)
One-period lagged utilization same make vehicle (thousands of miles)	0.281 (0.13)	Horsepower ÷ engine displacement (cubic inches) for households with heads 35 years old or younger	1.03 (1.46)
Two-period lagged utilization same make vehicle (thousands of miles)	0.0549 (0.117)	Luggage Space (cubic feet) for households with four members or more	0.0200 (0.0105)
Front and rear shoulder room (inches) for households with 2 members or fewer	0.0250 (0.00686)	New vehicle indicator (vehicle 2 years old or newer)	0.564 (0.291)
Front and rear shoulder room (inches) for households with 3 members or more	0.0516 (0.0136)	Old vehicle indicator (vehicle 8 years old or older)	−0.188 (0.225)

Source: Authors' calculations.

a. Dependent variable is the probability of choosing to own vehicle type i at time t (i denotes make, model, and vintage).

b. Standard errors are in parentheses. Log likelihood at zero is −838.1; log likelihood at convergence is −304.3.

c. Annual fuel cost is derived by multiplying fuel cost in dollars per mile by typical utilization in miles. Fuel cost is determined by dividing the prevailing price per gallon by vehicle fuel efficiency. Typical utilization is determined as 2,684 + 457.8 × number of household members + 0.0529 × annual income. The parameters in this equation were estimated by ordinary least squares by using average utilizations derived from all available periods in the household sample.

d. Capital cost is the vehicle's prevailing market value.

58   *Blind Intersection?*

Table 3-8. Type-Choice Model Estimates for Two-Vehicle Households[a]

Explanatory variable	Coefficient[b]	Explanatory variable	Coefficient[b]
Annual fuel cost of both		Pickup truck indicator	0.543
vehicles ÷ annual	−20.43		(0.414)
income (dollars)[c]	(8.44)	Number of American Motors	−0.520
Vehicles' capital cost ÷	−1.35	cars in portfolio	(0.465)
annual income (dollars)[d]	(0.469)	Number of Fords	−0.018
One-period lagged			(0.231)
utilization same vehicles	1.10	Number of Chryslers	−0.194
(thousands of miles)	(0.0749)		(0.263)
Two-period lagged		Number of foreign cars	−0.723
utilization same vehicles	0.108		(0.278)
(thousands of miles)	(0.00690)	Number of vehicles two	0.817
One-period lagged		years old or newer	(0.313)
utilization same make		Number of vehicles eight	−0.036
vehicles (thousands of	0.539	years old or older	(0.197)
miles)	(0.0810)		
Two-period lagged			
utilization same make			
vehicles (thousands of	−0.0933		
miles)	(0.0681)		
Front and rear shoulder	0.00781		
room summed (inches)	(0.00476)		

Source: Authors' calculations.

a. Dependent variable is the probability of choosing to own vehicle portfolio i in period t (i denotes combination of two vehicle types).

b. Standard errors are in parentheses. Log likelihood at zero is −833.5; log likelihood at convergence is −246.2. Number of observations is 362.

c. For definition of annual fuel cost, see table 3-7. Typical utilization of each vehicle is determined as $331 + 151.1 \times$ number of household members $+ 0.047 \times$ annual income.

d. Capital cost is vehicles' prevailing market value.

Table 3-9. Utilization Model Estimates for Single-Vehicle and Two-Vehicle Households[a]

Explanatory variable	Coefficient for single-vehicle household[b]	Coefficient for two-vehicle household[b]
Annual fuel cost[c]	−2.36	−0.923
	(1.70)	(0.846)
Annual income	−0.002	0.014
	(0.014)	(0.010)
One-period lagged utilization (miles) same vehicle(s)	0.363	0.392
	(0.032)	(0.029)
Two-period lagged utilization (miles) same vehicle(s)	0.310	0.014
	(0.041)	(0.030)
One-period lagged utilization (miles) same make vehicle(s)	0.416	0.238
	(0.448)	(0.077)
Two-period lagged utilization (miles) same make vehicle(s)	0.431	0.176
	(0.144)	(0.083)
Urban indicator (1 if urban location; 0 otherwise)	−399.4	38.3
	(313.1)	(252.6)
Northeast indicator (1 if northeastern U.S. location; 0 otherwise)	30.34	−3.40
	(306.8)	(283.4)
Age indicator (1 if head of household 50 years old or younger; 0 otherwise)	458.3	234.2
	(295.8)	(258.0)
Number of household workers	56.33	76.48
	(200.9)	(152.2)
New vehicle indicator (1 if newer vehicle of pair; 0 otherwise)	. . .	1355
	. . .	(233.7)
Constant	2077	249.9
	(540.6)	(583.8)
R^2	0.644	0.493
Number of observations	364	724

Source: Authors' calculations.
a. Dependent variable is accumulated vehicle miles traveled in period for each vehicle.
b. Standard errors are in parentheses.
c. Fuel cost and typical utilization are defined in tables 3-7 and 3-8.

Table 3-10. Parameter Estimates for Level-Choice Model[a]

Explanatory variable	Coefficient[b]
Number of household members[c]	0.247
	(0.071)
Number of household workers[c]	0.618
	(0.128)
Annual income (thousands of dollars)[c]	0.0199
	(0.00758)
Urban indicator (1 if urban location; 0 otherwise[c]	−0.565
	(0.206)
Log sum from type-choice models	0.389
	(0.046)
Choice indicator (1 if two-vehicle alternative; 0 otherwise)	−1.86
	(0.283)

Source: Authors' calculations.
a. Dependent variable is probability of choosing to own one or two vehicles.
b. Standard errors are in parentheses. Log likelihood at zero is −503.2; log likelihood at convergence is −369.5. Number of observations is 726.
c. Defined for two-vehicle alternative only.

CHAPTER FOUR

Economic Effects of Voluntary Export Restrictions

FRED MANNERING and CLIFFORD WINSTON

IN 1981, under the pressure of record financial losses in the automobile industry and the near bankruptcy of Chrysler Corporation, the U.S. government negotiated voluntary export restrictions with the Japanese government that limited total annual sales of new Japanese cars to 1.68 million vehicles (1980 Japanese retail passenger car sales in the United States had been 1.90 million vehicles).[1] In 1984 the restrictions were extended for another year, but the quota was raised to 1.85 million vehicles. Record profits in 1984 seemed to testify to the health of the U.S. industry, and the government allowed the restrictions to expire in March 1985. But apparently fearful of fanning the flames of protectionist sentiment in the White House and the Congress, the Japanese government decided in 1985 to limit the sales to 2.3 million vehicles. In 1987 the Japanese government announced that Japanese automakers would abide by the agreement until March 31, 1988.

The object of the restrictions has been to provide the U.S. automobile industry with time to retool and meet the Japanese challenge, thereby saving American jobs. The actual effects on consumers, automakers, and automobile workers, however, call into serious question the effectiveness of the restrictions in achieving their objective.

Conceptual Framework

Our discussion uses the automobile demand models presented in chapter 3 to assess whether consumers would have been economically

1. Motor Vehicle Manufacturing Association of the United States, *MVMA Motor Vehicle Facts & Figures '86* (Detroit: MVMA, 1986), p. 16.

better off with or without the restrictions.[2] Our analysis improves upon previous work by taking into account the effect of the restrictions on the prices of used vehicles, changes in vehicle quality mix and macroeconomic conditions, and shifts in consumers' choice of vehicle type in response to price changes induced by the restrictions.[3]

The first step in the comparison is calculating the prices of new and used U.S. and Japanese cars both with and without the restrictions. The prices of new cars with the restrictions are simply market prices in 1981–84; the prices of used cars for this period are estimated by the market

2. Formally, the change in welfare attributable to the restrictions is measured by compensating variations that indicate how much money a consumer would have to be given after a change in price or quality or both to be as well off as he was before the change. Given the logit automobile demand models presented in chapter 3, the compensating variations can be calculated using the formula presented by Kenneth A. Small and Harvey S. Rosen, "Applied Welfare Economics with Discrete Choice Models," *Econometrica*, vol. 49 (January 1981), pp. 105–30:

$$CV = -1/\lambda \left[\ln \sum_{i=1}^{n} \exp(V_i) \right]_{P_o}^{P_f},$$

where CV is the compensating variation, λ is the marginal utility of income, V_i is the mean (indirect) utility based on the vehicle type-choice specification given in appendix A to chapter 3 (which permits welfare calculations because it satisfies the condition that the demand for vehicle types is given by Roy's Identity), n is the number of vehicle types, and the square brackets indicate the difference in the expression inside when evaluated at prices of new and used U.S. and Japanese cars with no restrictions, P_o, and at prices of new and used U.S. and Japanese cars with restrictions, P_f.

In a logit model, the term in brackets equals the expected maximum utility obtainable from the available choices. The difference in utility from initial to final points is multiplied by the inverse of the marginal utility of income (that is, the dollars per unit of marginal utility) to yield a dollar value of the change in consumers' utility from the restrictions. Given our choice specifications for vehicle types (using Roy's Identity), the marginal utility of income, λ, equals minus the capital cost coefficient divided by household income.

3. Among the previous studies of the economic effects of the restrictions are José A. Gomez-Ibañez, Robert A. Leone, and Stephen A. O'Connell, "Restraining Auto Imports: Does Anyone Win?" *Journal of Policy Analysis and Management*, vol. 2, no. 2 (1983), pp. 196–219; David G. Tarr and Morris E. Morkre, *Aggregate Costs to the United States of Tariffs and Quotas on Imports: General Tariff Cuts and Removal of Quotas on Automobiles, Steel, Sugar, and Textiles*, Bureau of Economics staff report to the Federal Trade Commission (Government Printing Office, December 1984); Robert C. Feenstra, "Voluntary Export Restraints in U.S. Autos, 1980–81: Quality, Employment, and Welfare Effects," in Robert E. Baldwin and Anne O. Krueger, eds., *The Structure and Evolution of Recent U.S. Trade Policy* (University of Chicago Press, 1984); and Junichi Goto, "A General Equilibrium Analysis of Trade Restrictions under Imperfect Competition Theory and Some Evidence for the Automotive Trade," World Bank discussion paper no. DRD 130 (July 1985).

Table 4-1. Percentage Reduction in New Car Prices If Japanese Imports Had Not Been Restricted, 1981–84

Year	Japanese autos	U.S. autos[a]
1981	−0.1	0
1982	3.3	1.3
1983	17.3	6.9
1984	20.0	8.0

Source: Authors' calculations based on Robert W. Crandall, "Assessing the Impacts of the Automobile Voluntary Export Restraints upon U.S. Automobile Prices," paper presented to the Society of Government Economists, New York, December 1985.

a. Based on Crandall's estimate of conjectural elasticity of 0.4.

equilibrium model presented in chapter 3.[4] Calculations of what the prices of new U.S. and Japanese cars would have been in 1981–84 without the restrictions are based on an analysis by Robert Crandall.[5] Crandall developed a model to predict what new Japanese car prices in the United States would have been without restrictions, controlling for Japanese factor prices, exchange rates, vehicle option mix, and U.S. regulations on emissions. He then calculated the percentage increase in new Japanese car prices that could be attributed to the restrictions. Percentage increases in new U.S. car prices attributable to the restrictions were made by estimating the U.S. manufacturers' response to the Japanese car price increases—an elasticity of 0.4. The restrictions led to substantial price increases by both U.S. and Japanese automakers (table 4-1). By 1984 Japanese prices were roughly 20 percent higher than they would have been without the restrictions.

Estimates of what new car prices would have been if the restrictions had not been instituted can be made by reducing the actual new car prices in 1981–84 by the percentages given in table 4-1.[6] From these estimated prices, the equilibrium model estimates what used car prices and aggregate sales of U.S. and Japanese vehicles would have been without the restrictions. These predictions of average vehicle prices and total sales with and without the restrictions make it possible to calculate the change in U.S. and Japanese automakers' profits.

4. For new car prices see *Automotive News,* various issues 1981–84. Used car prices are predicted rather than actual to maintain consistency with the used car prices we must estimate for conditions not subject to restraints.

5. Robert W. Crandall, "Assessing the Impacts of the Automobile Voluntary Export Restraints upon U.S. Automobile Prices," paper presented to the Society of Government Economists, New York, December 1985.

6. Due to the absence of disaggregate estimates, we must assume these percentages apply uniformly to all vehicle types.

Estimates of the effects of the restrictions on U.S. automobile industry employment can be made using the U.S. labor demand function estimated in chapter 2. Because labor demand depends upon automobile output, these effects can be predicted by using output levels generated with and without the restrictions.

Results

Although international trade theory predicts that restricting free trade in imperfectly competitive industries, such as the automobile industry, will cause both domestic and foreign firms to raise their prices, it does not predict unambiguously what will happen to domestic firms' output.[7] One explanation is that trade restrictions allow domestic firms to raise prices because they know they will not lose sales to foreign firms. Thus the restrictions make the domestic firms' residual demand curve less elastic and induce them to equate marginal revenue and marginal cost at a higher price and a lower output than they would under free trade.[8] Alternatively, restrictions could cause an increase in domestic firms' residual demand, leading to an equilibrium at a higher price and higher output. In theory, then, trade restrictions can either increase or decrease domestic firms' output.

The estimated effect of the voluntary restrictions accepted by Japan has been a reduction in U.S. industry output from the levels that would have existed under unrestricted trade. As estimated in table 4-2, by 1984 industry output was reduced by roughly 300,000 vehicles.[9] Although cutting production at the very time Japanese competitors have agreed to curb sales may seem counterintuitive, the response is explained by the

7. See, for example, Kala Krishna, "Trade Restrictions as Facilitating Practices," Woodrow Wilson School discussion paper 55 (October 1983); and David Kreutzer, "Negative Output Response to Quota Protection" (unpublished paper, James Madison University, July 1985).

8. Because a change in elasticity will not influence domestic firms' output decisions under perfect competition, this explanation assumes an imperfectly competitive industry structure.

9. Although the price elasticities obtained from the logit type-choice models are reasonable (see appendix B to chapter 3), they do not reflect household changes in the number of vehicles owned in response to price changes and thus understate household total demand elasticities. The impact of quota-induced price increases on industry output is underestimated because for such increases output would fall further with more elastic demands.

Table 4-2. U.S. and Japanese Vehicle Sales and Average Prices with and without Trade Restrictions, 1982–84

Prices in current dollars

Item	1982	1983	1984
U.S. sales			
Restricted	5,803,632	6,703,788	7,548,168
Unrestricted	5,878,909	6,929,536	7,851,302
U.S. average new vehicle prices			
Restricted	9,742	10,248	10,713
Unrestricted	9,555	9,659	9,599
Japanese sales			
Restricted	1,848,329	1,922,937	1,912,249
Unrestricted	1,886,549	2,084,803	2,164,096
Japanese average new vehicle prices			
Restricted	7,952	8,462	9,574
Unrestricted	7,639	7,044	7,001

Source: Authors' calculations.

change in U.S. industry profits attributable to the restrictions. We estimate that by 1984 the restrictions led to an $8.9 billion increase in U.S. producers' profits, virtually all of the industry's record profits that year.[10] But the U.S. automakers were not alone in harvesting the benefits. Substantial vehicle price increases enabled the Japanese to earn at least an additional $3 billion in revenues by 1984.[11]

Estimates of the deadweight cost of the restrictions, that is, the difference between the loss to household vehicle owners and the gain in profits by automakers, are striking. By 1984, when the restrictions were binding very tightly, the welfare cost to household vehicle owners was roughly $14 billion, while automakers increased profits nearly $9 billion.[12]

10. The change in profits is determined by taking the estimated output response and the U.S. cost function in chapter 2 to determine the change in costs and by taking the estimated output and price response to determine the change in revenues.

11. The theoretical possibility of this result is discussed in Krishna, "Trade Restrictions as Facilitating Practices." The figure reported here represents a lower-bound gain in profits because total Japanese costs were reduced by the lower output. The Japanese automakers probably used the additional capacity caused by the restrictions for additional domestic or other foreign sales. Thus we cannot calculate the effect of the restrictions on Japanese industry profits in the same manner as we did for the U.S. industry.

12. Estimates of the cost to vehicle owners were obtained by the Small-Rosen formula using the household as our unit of measurement. This unit is used because the demand model estimated the vehicle purchasing decisions of households. In addition,

**Table 4-3. Estimated Change in U.S. Automobile Employment Attributable to
Voluntary Export Restrictions, 1982–84**

Year	Number of workers	Average industry wage (dollars)
1982	−7,265	34,323
1983	−23,448	35,473
1984	−31,754	37,007

Source: Authors' calculations.

Thus the deadweight loss to U.S. society from the restrictions ap-
proached $5 billion; it was less than $2 billion when more than $3 billion
in revenue gains to the Japanese are accounted for.[13]

This result may be somewhat disturbing to policymakers, but not so
disturbing as the impact of the restrictions on automobile employment.
As table 4-3 shows, the fall in U.S. automakers' output caused by the
increased vehicle prices associated with restrictions led to an estimated
loss in employment of more than 30,000 workers by 1984.[14] At the
average industry wage, such a cut would amount to more than a $1 billion
reduction in the total wage bill. To be sure, the average industry wage
has probably increased because of the restrictions, and workers who
were able to share the U.S. industry profits have received a benefit that
partially offsets this overall loss to labor. Further, increasing numbers

---

because the demand model is a probabilistic choice model, we must include all households
regardless of vehicles chosen or ownership levels. Aggregate estimates were obtained
by estimating the cost per household by ownership level and multiplying this figure by
the number of households in that ownership level. The cost of the restrictions for all
ownership levels was then tabulated. For households with no vehicles or with three or
more, we used the average welfare cost for one- and two-vehicle households, then
explored alternative welfare cost assumptions and found no significant qualitative
changes in our findings. Finally, this analysis assumes that households do not change
ownership levels in response to quota-induced price changes. This assumption is
reasonable given the relatively constant share of ownership levels during the past
decade. For example, the largest change in each ownership level from 1977 to 1983 was
less than 2.2 percent. The change in the number of households that do not own a vehicle
was 1.9 percent. See MVMA, *Motor Vehicle Facts & Figures '86,* p. 42.

13. Using a different methodology, Goto estimates the deadweight loss to U.S.
society from the restrictions to be $5.5 billion in 1984 dollars. See "General Equilibrium
Analysis of Trade Restrictions," p. 48. Because we do not account for the additional
gain to Japanese producers from lower costs, $2 billion represents an upper bound on
the U.S.-Japan deadweight loss. A world deadweight loss would have to include profits
to European producers generated by the restrictions.

14. As indicated in note 9, the loss in employment is actually understated by our
logit type choice models.

of Japanese automobile plants in the United States mean increasing U.S. automobile employment in some regions of the country, but this also means decreasing U.S. automobile employment in other regions of the country.[15] Thus these gains probably do not directly offset the losses.

Policy Implications

The object of the voluntary export restrictions was to help the U.S. automobile industry get back on its feet and to preserve American jobs. The restrictions may partially have succeeded because they enabled the industry to earn record profits, some of which may be used for investments that improve productivity and technology. But the restrictions have not saved American jobs, and American consumers have paid a heavy price. Worse, as argued in chapter 3, domestic firms may be hurt in the long run because foreign firms responded to trade protection by increasing their U.S. production capacity.

Although the current restrictions are not as tightly binding as the original sales limits, they nonetheless contribute to a deadweight loss and provide further incentives for Japanese firms to expand their U.S. production capacity. Ultimately, U.S. workers, consumers, and producers are likely to be hurt by the continuation of any form of automobile sales restraints.

15. Japanese firms have built most of their U.S. plants far from Detroit. Thus the additional employment generated will not accrue to people who were laid off because of the restrictions or who may be laid off because of increased competition.

CHAPTER FIVE

Recent Automobile Occupant Safety Proposals

FRED MANNERING and CLIFFORD WINSTON

MORE THAN 25,000 people die in automobile accidents in the United States every year, and hundreds of thousands more are injured. The related medical costs amount to several billion dollars a year; the wider costs to society, if they could be calculated, are surely far greater. Government policies at all levels have long been targeted at reducing these losses, but in the 1980s, state and federal proposals for regulating the safety of automobile occupants have focused on the use of seat belts and on the 55 mph speed limit.

Almost everyone agrees that deaths and injuries on the nation's highways and their associated medical costs would be reduced substantially if automobile drivers and passengers wore seat belts, but only 13 percent do so.[1] Similarly, the 55 mph speed limit has, since 1974, served to slow the mounting death toll, but compliance with the law has become increasingly lax in the 1980s. To counter these trends the Department of Transportation is urging the states to enact mandatory seat belt laws (in lieu of such automatic restraint systems as airbags or passive belts) and opposing any increase in the 55 mph limit.

Because they have important economic implications for consumers and automakers, these current federal proposals for regulating automobile safety on the nation's roads have generated considerable controversy. Consumers often contend that seat belts are uncomfortable, that they are time-consuming to put on and adjust, that passive restraints are

1. This figure is based on Department of Transportation observation studies taken before the passage of mandatory seat belt laws.

expensive and may not be effective, and that laws mandating belt use cannot be enforced. Automakers have consistently opposed mandatory passive restraints on grounds of cost and consumer resistance. The 55 mph speed limit has been criticized as unnecessary, particularly on rural stretches of interstate, and costly in its extension of driving time, especially on longer trips.

In this chapter we evaluate the social desirability of the policies advocated by the Department of Transportation.

Mandatory Seat Belt Laws

In the past decade the federal government has vigorously attempted to overcome public reluctance to wear seat belts. Under the Carter administration, the Department of Transportation issued regulations that would have required all 1984 model cars to be equipped with air bags or passive belts. The Reagan administration rescinded those regulations, but the Supreme Court ruled the action improper. In response Transportation Secretary Elizabeth Dole ruled in July 1984 that automatic restraints would be required in all cars manufactured after 1989 unless states accounting for two-thirds of the U.S. population passed laws mandating the use of seat belts.[2] Although many states have passed such laws, several of them seem not to meet federal criteria. Thus the regulation requiring automatic restraints is unlikely to be rescinded.[3]

In this section we analyze whether laws mandating seat belt use are in the public interest. We discuss the major hypotheses as to why voluntary seat belt use is so low, use these hypotheses to specify a model of the choice to use seat belts, estimate the economic cost of forced use

2. Under the initial ruling in standard 208, the minimum criteria for an acceptable seat belt law are:

—Each front seat occupant must be belted at all times; waivers are granted for medical reasons only.

—A minimum penalty for violating the law is $25.00 for each occupant (this may include court costs).

—Nonuse of a belt may mitigate damages.

—There must be a program to encourage compliance with the belt use laws.

—The effective date of any belt use law must be no later than September 1, 1989.

3. See Reginald Stuart, "Panel Rejects a Challenge to U.S. Plan to Drop Air Bag Rules," *New York Times*, September 19, 1986.

based on this choice model, and quantify the reductions in external costs from increased use.[4]

Causes of Low Levels of Seat Belt Use

Hypotheses about why so few people use seat belts abound. In most cases the explanations postulate rational objections to the belts, objections that can be put into an economic model that estimates the cost of forced use of seat belts and thus makes possible an evaluation of the cost-effectiveness of the Department of Transportation regulations. Although irrationality may enter into the decision to use a seat belt, it is difficult to provide an empirical basis for such behavior that can lead to useful policy guidance.[5]

There are four standard hypotheses for the general refusal to wear seat belts: that to do so is not cost-effective, that there is little probability of an accident, that there are other ways of maintaining safety, and that seat belts may not be effective in preventing injury.

An economist's instinctive explanation for the general refusal to wear seat belts is that it reflects individuals' balancing of the inconvenience of using the belts—the time required to fasten them and get comfortable, the time it takes to unfasten them—and perceived benefits from using them. This explanation is motivated, for example, by rough cost-benefit calculations carried out by Thaler and Rosen that suggest benefits from seat belt use—a reduced probability of death or injury from an accident— could be exceeded by the costs of the time needed to fasten and unfasten belts. This hypothesis suggests that comfort and the time spent fastening belts are important considerations in the decision to wear them.[6]

4. Previous cost-benefit analyses of seat belt use have been carried out by Lester Lave and Warren E. Weber, "A Benefit-Cost Analysis of Auto Safety Features," *Applied Economics*, vol. 2, no. 2 (1970), pp. 265–75; Richard Thaler and Sherwin Rosen, "The Value of Saving a Life: Evidence from the Labor Market," in Nestor E. Terleckyj, ed., *Household Production and Consumption Studies in Income and Wealth* (New York: Columbia University Press, 1975), pp. 265–301; and Glenn Blomquist, "Value of Life-Saving: Implications of Consumption Activity," *Journal of Political Economy*, vol. 87 (June 1979), pp. 540–58. The approach used here extends their analyses.

5. It might be argued that people are not irrational but that they do not have complete information about the effectiveness of seat belts, the likelihood of an accident, and so on. It would then be useful to test whether people would wear seat belts given complete information. While this approach may be worth pursuing, our analysis does not suggest that people are making uninformed judgments.

6. Throughout this chapter we assume that it takes no perceptible amount of time to release belts. The implication of this assumption is noted later.

Another possible determinant of seat belt use is that automobile occupants can never be certain whether they will be in an accident. If they draw on typical experience, they will probably conclude that the chance of having an accident is very low. Those who come to this conclusion do not use seat belts.[7] The extreme form of this hypothesis suggests that the probability of an injury-causing accident should have no effect on seat belt use because this probability is assumed to be zero by all automobile travelers.

Whether to wear a seat belt is only one of many choices people make to ensure their safety. Drivers and passengers who do not wear belts can compensate by making other choices that maintain this desired level of safety.[8] In this sense people purchase freedom from being vigilant about safety (that is, using seat belts) by buying medical insurance, driving larger and therefore presumably safer cars, or by altering driving behavior, although this last is difficult to quantify reliably. The hypothesis thus contends that safety-related attributes of a vehicle, such as weight, and the amount of an individual's medical insurance coverage influence seat belt use.

Individuals' beliefs about the effectiveness of seat belts can also affect their choices.[9] Given available information, people exercise some choice in their beliefs about the effectiveness of seat belts for reducing auto-related injuries that will ultimately govern their decision to use or not to use the belts. Individuals can also manipulate their beliefs about the effectiveness of seat belts—for instance, by continually referring to an episode in which someone was trapped by a seat belt—and ignore information on the effectiveness of wearing the belts. It is difficult, of course, to determine empirically whether beliefs are being manipulated, but the effect of beliefs about belts' effectiveness on their use can be analyzed.

These four hypotheses suggest that the specification of a seat belt choice model should control for the time it takes to fasten belts and their

7. See Richard J. Arnould and Henry Grabowski, "Auto Safety Regulation: An Analysis of Market Failure," *Bell Journal of Economics*, vol. 12 (Spring 1981), pp. 27–48.

8. See Lloyd D. Orr, "Incentives and Efficiency in Automobile Safety Regulation," *Quarterly Review of Economics and Business*, vol. 22 (Autumn 1982), pp. 43–65.

9. See George A. Akerlof and William T. Dickens, "The Economic Consequences of Cognitive Dissonance," *American Economic Review*, vol. 72 (June 1982), pp. 307–19, for an innovative paper on the effect of beliefs on choices that is applicable in the case of seat belt use.

comfort, the probability of being involved in an accident, vehicle weight and medical insurance coverage, and beliefs about the effectiveness of seat belts in preventing injury. The model we use to evaluate mandatory seat belt laws also controls for socioeconomic variables and driver characteristics.

Models and Sample

The choices in our analysis include seat belt use, beliefs about seat belt effectiveness, vehicle type, and vehicle use.[10] Models of vehicle-type choice and use will not be presented here, although the influence of these decisions on beliefs and seat belt use will be accounted for in the estimation of the seat belt use and beliefs models. The formal derivation of the beliefs and seat belt models is contained in appendix A to this chapter.[11]

The data used to estimate the models are from a telephone survey designed by the authors. (Although the Department of Transportation conducts similar surveys, it does not collect information on variables that relate to the hypotheses of interest here.) We obtained 310 responses based on a random September 1984 telephone survey of drivers in the Washington, D.C., and State College, Pennsylvania, areas. The mean annual household income of those surveyed was $31,667, and 76 percent of the respondents had some education beyond high school. Thus the drivers in the sample tended to be more affluent and better educated than the average driver in the United States. The proportion of the respondents that claimed to wear seat belts regularly, 32 percent, was, however, consistent with the responses in DOT's national surveys of reported seat belt usage, although the department has found that reported usage is considerably greater than observed usage. The average annual vehicle miles traveled by respondents was 14,075, while the national average is estimated as 14,152.[12]

Survey responses also showed that 75 percent of the drivers believed seat belts significantly improve their chances of surviving a serious accident, a figure consistent with DOT's national surveys and one suggesting that people are not manipulating themselves into beliefs that

10. For the remainder of this chapter, we will be concerned solely with drivers' seat belt usage behavior.

11. These models are specified as binary logit.

12. Department of Transportation National Travel Surveys.

justify not wearing seat belts. Finally, responses concerning seat belt systems appear to be reasonable. The reported mean time to fasten belts was 2.97 seconds (with a range of 2 to 6 seconds),[13] and 36 percent of the respondents found their seat belt system comfortable. Because we were unable to get reliable responses regarding drivers' medical insurance coverage, this aspect of the hypothesis that people take measures other than seat belt use to remain free from vigilance over their own safety could not be considered.

The survey results were supplemented with data on the attributes of respondents' vehicles. Vehicle weight was obtained from Consumer Reports;[14] the annual probability of an auto-related injury by specific make, model, and vintage was obtained from the Highway Loss Data Institute, Washington, D.C. To facilitate collection of this information, we restricted our sample to owners of vehicles manufactured since 1980. Sample means and standard deviations of all the variables are given with the estimation results in the next section, and the telephone survey questionnaire is reproduced in appendix B to this chapter.

Estimation

Beliefs about the effectiveness of seat belts were specified to be a function of socioeconomic characteristics (education, age, sex, presence of children, income) and driving experience and environment (accident experience, location of residence). The estimation results, presented in table 5-1, indicate that the presence of children in a household or residence in areas requiring commuting and intercity driving increase belief in seat belt effectiveness. In general, women believe more strongly than men, older people less strongly than other age groups, that belts are effective. Increased levels of education or experience of a serious accident also have a positive effect.

Based on these parameter estimates, we obtained a predicted beliefs variable and incorporated it with variables related to the other three hypotheses (that use is related to the time it takes to fasten belts and belt comfort, vehicle weight, and probability of auto injury), socioeconomic

13. These figures are consistent with evidence in Blomquist, "Value of Life-Saving." The sample mean time to fasten belts for seat belt users and nonusers was not statistically significantly different because there was a considerable overlap of the responses.

14. *Consumer Reports Automotive Annual* (New York: Consumer Reports, various years).

Table 5-1. Maximum Likelihood Parameter Estimates of Beliefs Model and Sample Means

Variable	Estimate[a]	Sample mean[b]
Belief indicator (1 if believe seat belts significantly increase chances of surviving a serious accident; 0 otherwise)	. . .	0.75
Constant	−0.013	. . .
	(1.148)	. . .
Education indicator (1 if at least some beyond high school; 0 otherwise)	1.37	0.761
	(0.423)	. . .
Age	−0.037	35.39
	(0.025)	(10.63)
Number of children less than 16 years old	1.184	0.655
	(0.399)	(0.724)
Location indicator (1 if live in rural or suburban location; 0 if live in urban location)	1.96	0.668
	(0.388)	. . .
Annual household income (thousands of dollars)	0.0205	31.677
	(0.0216)	(11.282)
Sex indicator (1 female; 0 male)	0.936	0.40
	(0.465)	. . .
Serious accident indicator (1 if no serious accidents within last 3 years; 0 otherwise)	−0.934	0.816
	(0.807)	. . .

Source: Authors' calculations.
a. Standard errors in parentheses. Number of observations = 310; log likelihood at zero = −214.87; log likelihood at convergence = −97.56; likelihood ratio index = .546; 87 percent correctly predicted.
b. Standard deviations in parentheses.

variables (age), and driving-experience variables (accident experience, annual vehicle miles traveled) to specify a seat belt use model. The parameter estimates are given in table 5-2, and seat belt choice elasticities are presented in table 5-3.[15] As table 5-3 shows, age, annual driving mileage, and accident experiences all have a positive and important influence on seat belt use. Time required to fasten belts has a significant negative effect on belt use and a very large elasticity. Because of the relatively low statistical significance of and elasticity for comfort, time required to fasten them appears to be the onerous aspect of belt use. The

15. Additional models were estimated to investigate how trip distance and weather conditions affected the determinants of belt use. As expected, reported belt use increased when weather conditions were poor and fell for short trips. However, the main results derived from the key parameters in the model did not change for particular driving conditions or trip distance.

A seat belt choice elasticity with respect to a given variable can be interpreted as the percentage change in the probability of wearing a seat belt that results from a 1 percent change in the given variable.

Table 5-2. Maximum Likelihood Parameter Estimates of Seat Belt Usage Model and Sample Means

Variable	Estimate[a]	Sample mean[b]
Seat belt indicator (1 if wear belts regularly; 0 otherwise)	. . .	0.33
Constant	11.078	. . .
	(6.737)	. . .
Age	0.079	35.39
	(0.038)	(10.63)
Time to fasten belts (seconds)[c]	−2.82	2.97
	(0.542)	(0.99)
Serious accident indicator (1 if no serious accidents within last 3 years; 0 otherwise)	−1.84	0.816
	(0.558)	. . .
Vehicle weight (pounds)[d]	−0.0060	2819.81
	(0.0023)	(166.16)
Annual vehicle miles traveled[e]	0.00038	14,075.3
	(0.00021)	(2,625.4)
Estimated belief in probability of seat belt effectiveness[f]	3.305	0.71
	(2.851)	
Annual probability of auto-related injury (percent) if annual household income is less than $35,000; 0 otherwise[g]	1.198	1.21
	(0.340)	(0.98)
Comfort indicator (1 if seat belt system is comfortable; 0 otherwise)	0.782	0.36
	(0.531)	. . .

Source: Authors' calculations.

a. Standard errors in parentheses. Number of observations = 310; log likelihood at zero = −214.87; log likelihood at convergence = −63.65; likelihood ratio index = .704; 92.6 percent correctly predicted.

b. Standard deviations in parentheses.

c. As noted in the text, it is unlikely that this variable is being manipulated by respondents.

d. Because choice of vehicle type and seat belt use are interrelated, vehicle weight is endogenous. Thus we used the expected value of vehicle weight to obtain a consistent estimate. This is obtained by estimating a vehicle type choice model and calculating $E(weight) = \Sigma_i P_i \times weight_i$, where P_i is the probability of the household owning vehicle type i and $weight_i$ is the weight of vehicle type i.

e. Because choice of vehicle type and vehicle use are interrelated, vehicle miles traveled must be considered endogenous in the seat belt use model. To deal with this endogeneity, we regress vehicle miles traveled on socioeconomic variables and use the predicted value in the seat belt model.

f. The value used here is the probability that households believe seat belts are effective, as obtained from the beliefs model presented in table 5-1.

g. The treatment of the annual probability of an auto-related injury, which is vehicle-specific, parallels the treatment of vehicle weight described in note d. Initial estimations revealed that the seat belt use decisions of households with annual incomes exceeding $35,000 were insensitive to the degree of their vehicle's injury protection. We speculate that this is due to the uniformly high levels of safety provided by vehicles (Volvos, Lincolns, and so on) typically owned by this population segment. Finally, the construction of this variable controls for the mix of drivers.

very large elasticity for vehicle weight supports the hypothesis that safety can be a function of alternatives to belt use.

There is less support for the hypotheses that low use is determined primarily by the extent of belief in the ineffectiveness of seat belts or that it is determined by the lack of fear of an accident. The statistical significance of the beliefs variable is marginal, and although its elasticity exceeds 1.0, it is not as large as many of the other estimated responses.

Table 5-3. Seat Belt Usage Elasticities[a]

Variable	Elasticity
Age	1.88
Time to fasten seat belt	−5.64
Experience of having any serious accidents within the past three years	−1.00
Vehicle weight	−11.42
Annual vehicle miles traveled	3.60
Belief probability of seat belt effectiveness	1.58
Annual probability of auto-related injury	0.97
Comfort	0.19

Source: Authors' calculations.

a. Because the "comfort" and "serious accident" variables are restricted to assume values of either zero or one, some caution should be exercised in interpreting their elasticities.

The annual probability of an auto-related injury has a significant positive coefficient and an elasticity of 0.97—direct evidence that drivers are somewhat sensitive to the likelihood of an auto accident. This conclusion is, of course, based on a variable constructed from objective data generated by the Highway Loss Data Institute and not a variable based on drivers' actual perceptions of their likelihood of being in an accident. Unfortunately, econometric analysis based on this more direct information is difficult and potentially inconclusive.[16] Nonetheless, the results suggest that the hypothesis of public insensitivity to the probability of being in an accident does not explain low levels of belt use.

Cost-Benefit Considerations

From the foregoing results we estimated the net benefits of mandatory seat belt use. Based primarily on the value that drivers place on the time to fasten belts, the total cost of seat belt use over the duration of vehicle ownership is $6,442.[17] The cost for each trip, $0.38, reflects the high

16. Because of a lack of variation in the responses, one could find that the coefficient for perceived probabilities is statistically insignificant, although the reported probabilities were substantially greater than zero. In addition, eliciting thoughtful perceptions in a telephone survey of the likelihood of being in an auto accident is difficult.

17. These costs are estimated in the following indirect way because our seat belt use equation does not facilitate a direct calculation of the trade-off between money and time. From a vehicle-type choice model based on the earlier model by Mannering and Winston we find that the marginal rate of substitution between vehicle weight and capital costs is $4.62 a pound. From the seat belt model we find that the marginal rate of substitution between vehicle weight and time to fasten belts is 0.00213 seconds a pound (the same sample was used for the seat belt and vehicle-type choice models). The ratio

disutility drivers attach to fastening their seat belts.[18]

In a 1984 paper, which contains estimates of consumers' willingness to pay for improvements in automobile safety based on their vehicle choices, we found that drivers' valuation of a 1 percent reduction in the conditional probability of a severe accident given the occurrence of an accident over the life of vehicle ownership was $245.30.[19] Multiplying this figure by the true reduction in this probability attributable to seat belt use (21.4 percent assuming a 100 percent rate of use) yields a benefit from seat belt use over the life of vehicle ownership of $5,249, or a

---

of these marginal rates of substitution, $4.62 a pound divided by 0.00213 seconds a pound, yields a value of the time to fasten belts over the duration of vehicle ownership of $2,169 a second. Multiplying this by the sample mean time to fasten belts, 2.97 seconds, yields the figure in the text. To the extent that releasing belts takes a perceptible amount of time, this figure understates the total cost of seat belt use.

18. This figure of $0.38 is obtained by dividing the cost of seat belt use over the duration of vehicle ownership by the total number of trips. The Department of Transportation estimates the average number of automobile trips a year to be 1,697; see Federal Highway Administration, *Household Travel: 1977 Nationwide Personal Transportation Study* (Department of Transportation, July 1982). The length of vehicle ownership is conservatively estimated (from a seat belt cost estimation perspective) to be ten years, which is slightly less than the median life of a vehicle. Thus $6,442 divided by 16,970 trips equals $0.38 a trip.

Transportation economists have often found very high values of time for activities that pertain to specific components of a trip—for example, the value of a businessman's time between departures in a bus terminal, the value of a shipper's time for shipments of perishable commodities by railroad, and the value of the time a commuter takes to walk to a transit stop. See Clifford Winston, "Conceptual Developments in the Economics of Transportation: An Interpretive Survey," *Journal of Economic Literature*, vol. 23 (March 1985), pp. 57–94, for specific estimates. The explanation for these high valuations of time is not the individuals' opportunity cost of time, but the high disutility they attach to time spent in these activities. Accordingly, the results presented here suggest that drivers attach extremely high disutility to the activity of fastening their seat belts.

It is, however, misleading to express the disutility that drivers attach to fastening belts in terms of an hourly value of time. One can easily think of pleasurable and unpleasurable activities that only take a few seconds but whose hourly valuation would be extremely high. The aggregation of such activities to estimate an hourly valuation involves an implausible linearity assumption. For example, the valuation of fastening a belt consecutively for an hour (the usual way an activity's hourly value is characterized) is unlikely to be the same as the valuation of an hour of fastening a belt over many years.

19. Clifford Winston and Fred Mannering, "Consumer Demand for Automobile Safety," *American Economic Review*, vol. 74 (May 1984), pp. 316–19. By basic probability theory, this conditional probability can be expressed as $\text{Prob}(S/A) = \text{Prob}(S \text{ intersection } A) \div \text{Prob}(A)$, where S denotes a severe accident (as defined by the National Highway Traffic Safety Administration's Abbreviated Injury Scale) and A denotes an accident of any severity.

benefit per trip of roughly $0.31.[20] Net private costs to drivers of mandatory seat belt laws amount to $0.07 cents a trip, or an annual cost of $11.8 billion in 1984 dollars.[21]

The net private costs of mandatory seat belt laws must be balanced against the benefits of reductions in external costs. The costs associated with automobile injuries and fatalities that could be reduced by compulsory seat belt laws include reductions in the tax base, insurance expenses, productivity losses, and medical costs (particularly follow-on home care). Although mandatory seat belt laws reduce these annual costs by an estimated $2.96 billion in 1984 dollars, the benefits do not offset the increase in private costs.[22] On balance, mandatory seat belt laws do not appear justified on cost-benefit grounds.

Policy Implications

To some extent the lack of an immediate net benefit from a law requiring the use of seat belts is not surprising. Automobile occupants have long revealed their preferences: not one in seven has regularly chosen to wear a seat belt. A law that makes wearing seat belts compulsory is, then, not likely to be socially desirable unless there are substantial external benefits.[23] Several qualifications, however, are in

20. This estimate is internally consistent with the results obtained here. Benefits can be estimated here as the willingness to pay for reductions in absolute accident probabilities. Because this probability applied to a truncated sample, we elected not to use it as a basis for our primary benefits estimate. However, a comparison of the two approaches, based on plausible assumptions, yielded comparable benefits estimates.

21. Because costs and benefits are expressed per trip, the estimate of net benefits per trip is unaffected by alternative values of the length of vehicle ownership and the number of trips a year. The figure of $11.8 billion is obtained by multiplying the net cost per trip ($0.07) by the average number of a driver's trips a year (1,697) by the number of U.S. drivers (a conservative estimate is 100 million; the number of licensed drivers exceeds this figure).

22. This estimate is obtained by multiplying the cost per person of a particular externality by the reduction in the number of injuries and fatalities from increased seat belt use. Externality costs are from National Highway Traffic Safety Administration, *The Economic Cost to Society of Motor Vehicle Accidents* (Department of Transportation, 1983). Externalities include police costs, insurance administration costs, welfare and public assistance administration costs, tax-base reduction, employer retraining costs, and medical costs such as home modification, second-year unique services, and follow-on care. The reduction in the number of injuries and fatalities from increased seat belt use is from Arnould and Grabowski, "Auto Safety Regulation."

23. Indeed, as this book goes to press, voters in Nebraska and Massachusetts have repealed their states' mandatory seat belt laws. Similar repeal drives could occur in other states that now have the laws.

order. Our calculations do not include emotional costs borne by those who survive an accident victim, costs that are not compensated by insurance settlements. Reductions in these costs, which are very difficult to quantify, would contribute to the social desirability of seat belt laws.[24] Also, our analysis is based on preferences toward seat belt use developed before the passage of seat belt laws. Once in the habit of using belts, individuals could place a lower value on the time needed to fasten them that could persist even if the laws were rescinded.

Notwithstanding these qualifications, our results raise serious questions about the social desirability of the mandatory laws and suggest that alternative safety policies should be considered. One way to eliminate the cost of forcing people to use belts, while possibly achieving comparable benefits and preserving their freedom of choice, is to require automakers to install detachable passive belts or air bags. With only a 60 percent rate of passive belt use, the net benefits would be $5 billion annually.[25] With 20 percent of vehicle occupants using lap belts, the annual benefits from air bags are, depending on assumptions regarding installment costs, $2.4 billion to $6.2 billion.

To be sure, these findings are not based on observed behavior as in the case of the findings on seat belt use but rather on estimates of the effectiveness of these devices and estimates of people's willingness to pay for this effectiveness.[26] Because estimates of effectiveness based on observed behavior may not be as high as these estimates, net benefits may be overestimated. Indeed, this appears to be the case, because the demand for passive restraints is so small. It is not clear, however, that people's responses are based on adequate information. Safety advocates claim automakers have long been unwilling to market these devices aggressively, while surveys indicate that popular support for automatic restraints is just starting to develop.[27]

As such, the regulation proposed under the Carter administration that required automobiles to be equipped with either passive belts or air bags

24. Seat belt laws may also lead to increased driver risk-taking that leads to offsetting increases in injuries and fatalities. See Sam Peltzman, "The Effects of Automobile Safety Regulation," *Journal of Political Economy*, vol. 83 (August 1975), pp. 677–725.

25. Winston and Mannering, "Consumer Demand for Automobile Safety," p. 318. These estimates do not include externality cost reductions.

26. The benefit estimates for the seat belt analysis were obtained by this procedure, but corroborated by estimates based on choice behavior (see note 20).

27. See, for example, "Americans Back Air Bag Requirement," *Washington Post National Weekly Edition*, July 8, 1985.

would generate greater net benefits than the current policy of encouraging mandatory state seat belt laws. Using comparable estimation procedures, the requirement of passive belts or air bags generates at least the same benefits as mandatory seat belt laws but, by eliminating inconvenience costs for drivers and replacing them with manufacturers' installation costs, achieves these benefits at lower social cost. Subject to the qualifications noted above, the apparent failure of state seat belt laws to supersede the requirement that cars be equipped with automatic restraints appears to be in the public interest.

Recently, there have been some signs that the market may finally solve the occupant safety issue. Ford has offered air bags as options in its 1986 Tempo and Topaz compacts, while Mercedes-Benz installed driver-side air bags in all its 1986 models. General Motors will offer air bags as options in its 1988 model cars. After all the excitement, automobile occupant safety may be improved without government intervention.

The 55 MPH Speed Limit

At the height of the 1973 energy crisis, Congress imposed a national 55 mph speed limit to conserve energy. A perhaps unexpected benefit of this action has been a reduction in fatalities and serious injuries sustained in automobile accidents. Notwithstanding these safety gains, recent declines in the price of fuel and driver frustration with the lower legal speed have generated pressure to raise the national speed limit at least on lightly traveled rural roads. (Observers claim that the limit has in effect already been raised in those states that do not effectively enforce the 55 mph limit.) Transportation Secretary Dole has opposed any such increases.

A number of studies have evaluated the desirability of the 55 mph limit, but no consensus has emerged.[28] A comprehensive evaluation of the existing limit by the National Research Council has, however, assembled valuable data that could be used in a cost-benefit analysis.[29]

28. These studies are surveyed and critiqued by Ted R. Miller, "Evaluating the 55 MPH Speed Limit and Willingness to Pay for Reductions in Deaths and Injuries" (unpublished paper, Urban Institute, April 1984).

29. National Research Council, *55: A Decade of Experience*, Transportation Research Board special report 204 (Washington, D.C.: National Academy Press, 1984).

These data include the effect of the lower limit on hours of automobile and truck travel, fuel consumption, and fatalities and serious injuries. We use these data and a new estimate of the value of high-speed automobile travel time to determine the dollar valuation of life that justifies the 55 mph limit as compared with the original speed limits set by states, which were generally 65 mph and above.[30]

The primary costs of the 55 mph speed limit are the additional passenger hours of travel multiplied by the value of travelers' time.[31] The National Research Council estimates that the 55 mph limit led to 1.04 billion additional annual hours of travel for the occupants of cars and light trucks, commercial trucks, and buses.[32] We estimated the value of high-speed automobile travel time using a multinomial logit model of the choice of highway driving speed. The choices, 55 mph or less, 55 mph to 60 mph, 60 mph to 65 mph, and above 65 mph, are specified as a function of trip time, trip cost, the presence of passengers, and the driver's age, sex, and residence. The model is estimated using data generated by an interview survey (see appendix B to this chapter) of 301 drivers in Pittsburgh and State College, Pennsylvania, in the summer of 1985, a sample that seemed representative of highway drivers. Maximum likelihood parameter estimates of the model are given in table 5-4. The parameters are statistically reliable and of plausible sign, and the model appears to do a good job of explaining the choice of driving speed. The value of travel time per vehicle is obtained by dividing the coefficient of trip time by the coefficient of trip cost, which yields a value of $9.57 an hour. Dividing this figure by the average number of occupants per vehicle gives a value of travel time per traveler of $3.76 an hour.[33] Thus, the time

---

30. An evaluation for specific types of roads, such as lightly traveled rural roads, cannot be carried out because of the unavailability of data needed to estimate such key parameters as the value of travel time on these roads.

31. Our analysis does not include costs associated with the reduction of trips caused by the 55 mph limit, but this effect is likely to be small. See, for example, the automobile travel time elasticities in Steven A. Morrison and Clifford Winston, "An Econometric Analysis of the Demand for Intercity Passenger Transportation," *Research in Transportation Economics*, vol. 2 (1985), pp. 213–37.

32. National Research Council, *55: A Decade of Experience*, p. 119. Most of this travel is captive to a particular transportation mode.

33. Morrison and Winston, "Demand for Intercity Passenger Transportation," estimate the hourly value of travel time for automobile pleasure trips to be $1.12 in 1985 dollars. The estimate reported here is higher because it includes the value of time for work-related trips. One might question whether it is reasonable for the value of automobile travel time to be so much lower than the value of an individual's seat belt fastening

Table 5-4. Multinomial Logit Speed-Choice Estimates

Variable	Coefficient[a]
Trip time (hours)[b]	−1.167
	(0.497)
Driver age dummy, 1 if greater than 60; 0 otherwise	1.065
(defined for first alternative)[c]	(0.422)
Age of driver (defined for third and fourth alternatives)[c]	−0.073
	(0.013)
Passenger dummy, 1 if passenger present; 0 otherwise	−0.713
(defined for third and fourth alternatives)[c]	(0.326)
Sex of driver, 1 if male; 0 otherwise	1.339
(defined for fourth alternative)[c]	(0.518)
Residence dummy, 1 if rural; 0 otherwise	−0.676
(defined for third and fourth alternatives)[c]	(0.312)
Trip cost (dollars)[d]	−0.122
	(0.066)
Alternative 1 dummy[c]	−1.448
	(0.707)
Alternative 2 dummy[c]	−0.282
	(0.676)
Alternative 3 dummy[c]	1.819
	(0.482)

Source: Authors' calculations.

a. Standard errors are in parentheses. Number of observations = 310; log likelihood at zero = −417.27; log likelihood at convergence = −316.46.

b. Trip length divided by reported speed.

c. Alternatives are (1) 55 mph or less, (2) 55–60 mph, (3) 60–65 mph, (4) 65 mph or greater.

d. Trip cost includes fuel consumption and expected speeding costs. For a given speed, expected speeding costs include the probability of getting a ticket times the ticket cost plus the increase in insurance.

cost in 1985 dollars of the 55 mph limit is $3.91 billion ($3.76 an hour × 1.04 billion hours).[34] The National Research Council estimates the enforcement and compliance costs of the 55 mph limit to be $129.6 million in 1985 dollars, which pushes the total cost of the 55 mph limit to $4.04 billion.[35]

The benefits of the 55 mph limit are the $195 million reduction in direct costs from motor vehicle accidents, $70 million in program savings, and $3.02 billion in fuel savings, which yields a total benefit, exclusive of the benefits associated with reduced fatalities and serious injuries, of $3.26

time, but this result simply implies that people find it more onerous to spend time fastening belts than driving on interstate highways. Economic theory does not require the values of time for all automobile-related activities to be comparable.

34. This estimate is conservative because it probably understates the value of time for truck drivers. Their passenger hours, however, represent only 17 percent of total passenger hours; see National Research Council, *55: A Decade of Experience*, p. 113.

35. Ibid., p. 103. Some of these costs are offset by revenues from speeding fines.

billion in 1985 dollars.[36] To determine whether the 55 mph limit should be maintained, we ask what value of an individual's willingness to pay for a 1 percent reduction in the probability of death or serious disability from an accident over the remainder of his life would equate the benefits and costs of the 55 mph limit? We find this value to be $4,000, which implies a value of life of $400,000.[37] Because most estimates of the value of life exceed this figure, the continuation of the 55 mph limit at the national level is justified.[38]

It is natural to ask that if the 55 mph limit is in the national interest, why isn't the limit regularly obeyed? Recall our conclusion is that the current limit is socially beneficial as compared with the speed limits set by states. The average driving speed during the last year the state limits were in effect was 65 mph.[39] This does not imply that 55 mph is the optimal national limit or even superior to the previous state limits set for certain types of roads. However, given that the average speed on rural interstates is 59 mph, our conclusion is not necessarily inconsistent with observed driving behavior.[40] Nonetheless, attention should be given to the desirability of retaining the limit for certain roads such as lightly traveled interstates.[41] A number of states apparently believe that the current limit is inappropriate for these roads and have curtailed their

36. Ibid., pp. 91, 103, 107. The average price of gasoline in 1985 was $1.18 a gallon.

37. The $4,000 value is obtained as follows: exclusive of the benefits from reduced accidents, the costs of the 55 mph limit exceed the benefits by roughly $800 million. The speed limit is credited by the National Research Council with reducing the probability of a serious accident or fatality by 50 percent and with saving 4,000 lives a year. Thus $800 million in benefits is generated if an individual's willingness to pay for a 1 percent reduction in the probability of a serious accident or fatality is $4,000 ($4,000 for each 1 percent reduction × 50 percent × 4,000 lives = $800 million).

38. At an average gasoline price of $0.90 a gallon, the value of life that justifies continuation of the 55 mph limit is $750,000, which is still below most estimates of the value of life. A comprehensive survey of value of life estimates is contained in Ted R. Miller, Kenneth A. Reinert, and Brooke E. Whiting, *Alternative Approaches to Accident Cost Concepts* (U.S. Department of Transportation, Federal Highway Administration, January 1984).

39. National Research Council, *55: A Decade of Experience*, p. 3.

40. Ibid. This argument is subject to the effects of enforcement. The figure for the sample used here to estimate the value of time is 60 mph.

41. Although he does not provide any estimates of net benefit, Dana B. Kamerud has developed a parametric framework to assess the desirability of the 55 mph limit for different types of roads. However, among other deficiencies, his framework keeps the value of travel time constant over all types of roads. This approach is likely to generate misleading conclusions. See "The 55 MPH Speed Limit: Costs, Benefits, and Implied Trade-Offs," *Transportation Research*, vol. 17A, no. 1 (1983), pp. 51–64.

enforcement of it. Such bad social policy adds further motivation for considering the adoption of more finely tuned speed limits.[42]

Appendix A: Derivation of Binary Logit Models for Beliefs and Seat Belt Use

This appendix derives the beliefs and seat belt use models estimated in the text. We use the following notation:

let Y = income.

Cs = cost of seat belt use (time, discomfort costs).

S = 1 if seat belt is used; 0 otherwise.

Ca = expected accident (personal injury) costs without using a seat belt. These account for the probability of an accident and for insurance coverage.

B = Perceived percentage of expected accident costs if belt is used. If this beliefs variable is discrete (as it is in our empirical work) then it is equal to 100 percent if belts are believed ineffective and 0 percent if belts are believed effective.[43]

ϵ = costs of a perception (beliefs) error (for example, unnecessary expenses from an accident because of poor judgment or unanticipated accident costs).

α = parameters.

Z = explanatory variables (socioeconomic characteristics, vehicle attributes, driving activities and experience, and so forth).

η = unobserved variables.

Assuming that the individual maximizes his indirect utility function with respect to his choice of whether to wear a belt, S, and his belief about seat belt effectiveness, B, the individual's indirect utility function, V, can be written as

$$V = \underset{S,B}{\text{Max}} [Y - CsS - CaBS - \epsilon - (1 - S)Ca - \alpha Z - \eta].$$

42. As this book goes to press, the Senate has passed a bill that gives states the option of raising the speed limit to 65 mph on rural interstates.

43. Some people believe that wearing seat belts increases accident costs. In this case, the value of B would exceed 100 percent.

The individual's choice of S and B, which maximize V, can be derived by Roy's Identity:

$$S = \frac{-\partial V \,|\, \partial Cs}{\partial V \,|\, \partial Y} = 1 \text{ if seat belt is used, 0 otherwise.}$$

$$B = \frac{-\partial V \,|\, \partial Ca}{\partial V \,|\, \partial Y} \cdot \psi, \text{ where } \psi = 1 \text{ if } S = 1, B \text{ if } S = 0.$$

To specify a statistical model using this framework, we first note that because we are concerned with analyzing the determinants of discrete choices derived from a random utility function (B is now explicitly taken to be discrete), it is natural to express the likelihood of these events in terms of probabilities. Following standard procedure, if we assume η is distributed according to the extreme value distribution, we can specify a logit model of seat belt use and a logit model of beliefs. Because these choices are derived from the same indirect utility function, V, they will be interrelated through common unobservable components. From an econometric perspective, this interrelationship indicates that beliefs, which we hypothesize influence seat belt use, must be treated as endogenous.[44] Thus we specify the choice of beliefs as binary logit and include estimated beliefs probabilities as an explanatory variable in the binary logit choice model to obtain a consistent estimate of the effect of beliefs on seat belt use.[45] Formally, the beliefs logit model is specified as $P_B = 1/(1 + e^{-V_B})$, and the seat belt logit model as $P_S = 1/(1 + e^{-[V_S + \theta \hat{P}_B]})$, where V_B and V_S are components of the indirect utility function that relate to the choice of B and S, $\hat{P}_B$ is the estimated beliefs probability, and θ is a parameter.

---

44. It might be argued that beliefs are influenced by seat belt use. Such a model proved unsuccessful in attempts at specifying a nested-logit model of beliefs and belt use (log sums were not well-behaved.) In addition, sample responses indicated that beliefs were not manipulated to maintain consistency with decisions about belt use. Specifying beliefs as a function of belt use and belt use as a function of beliefs would yield two conditional probabilities that do not lead to a joint probability.

45. This procedure requires the explanatory variables in the beliefs model to be exogenous.

Appendix B: Seat Belt Usage and Highway Driving Speed
Surveys

Telephone Interview for Seat Belt Usage Sample

1. Do you own a 1980 or newer car? Yes _____No _____
   If yes, proceed with the rest of the questions.
2. How old are you? _____
3. What is your educational level?
   _____Some high school
   _____High-school graduate
   _____Vocational or technical school
   _____Some college
   _____College graduate
   _____Post-graduate work
4. Please estimate your total household annual income ($).
   _____5,000 or less
   _____5,000–14,999
   _____15,000–24,999
   _____25,000–34,999
   _____35,000–44,999
   _____45,000–49,999
   _____50,000 or over
5. What is the make, year, and model of the car you drive?
6. Do you wear seat belts regularly? No _____ Yes _____
7. How often do you wear seat belts when driving on roads that are
   wet, or snow- and ice-covered?
   _____Always
   _____Most of the time
   _____Sometimes
   _____Never
8. How often do you wear seat belts when driving on long trips?
   (Same ratings as question 7.)
9. How often do you wear seat belts when driving on short trips?
   (Same ratings as question 7.)
10. On a scale of 1 to 3, with 1 being "uncomfortable" and 3 being
    "comfortable," how would you rate the seat belt system in your
    car?
11. On a scale of 1 to 3, with 1 being "inconvenient" and 3 being
    "convenient," how would you rate the seat belt system in your car?

12. How would you describe the area in which you live?
    _____Urban
    _____Suburban
    _____Rural
13. What is the number of your household members?
14. What is the number of children of 16 years of age or less that you have?
15. How much time do you estimate it takes you to fasten your seat belt?
16. Have you had any serious accidents in the past 3 years?
    _____Yes _____No
17. How many miles do you drive per year?
18. How do you believe safety belts affect your chance of surviving a serious accident?
    _____Greatly improve survival
    _____Significantly improve survival
    _____No effect on survival
    _____Decreases chances of survival

Highway Driving Questionnaire

1. Recall a recent highway trip driven mainly on roads with a 55 mph speed limit that had a one-way trip length over 100 miles. Approximately what was the trip length? _____miles
2. How many passengers were in the car including yourself? _____
3. What average speed did you drive? 55 mph or less_____ 55–60 mph 60–65 mph_____ 65 or more_____.
4. Have you had any speeding tickets in the past 2 years? Yes_____ No_____
5. Have you had any serious accidents in the past 3 years? Yes_____ No_____
6. Do you wear seat belts? Never _____ Occasionally _____ Always _____
7. Do you believe seat belts are effective? Yes_____ No_____
8. What is your estimated highway miles per gallon of the car? _____
9. How many miles per year do you drive? _____
10. What is the make, model, and year of the car you drive? _____

11. What is your age? _____
12. How many years of school have you completed?
    Less than 12 years _____ High-school graduate _____
    Some college _____ College graduate _____ Vocational
    or technical school _____ Post-graduate work _____
13. What is your total household annual income?
    $20,000 or less _____
    $20,000 to $40,000 _____
    $40,000 or more _____
14. How many members are in your household? _____
15. How many members of your family are 16 years of age
    or under? _____
16. How would you classify the area in which you live?
    Urban _____ Rural _____
17. What is your sex? Male _____ Female _____

CHAPTER SIX

Expectations and Automobile Policy

DENNIS SHEEHAN and CLIFFORD WINSTON

CHAPTERS 4 and 5 have provided evidence that such federal government automobile policies as voluntary export restrictions for Japanese vehicles and mandatory seat belt laws have damaged the welfare of U.S. society. In addition, previous research has questioned the social desirability of the initial automobile emissions standards and automobile safety regulations.[1] Why, then, given their ineffectiveness, were these policies ever supported?

This chapter attempts to answer this question by analyzing the passage of legislation affecting automobile safety, emissions, and fuel economy. We develop a simple model of the determinants of voting, in which the probability of a legislator's voting for automobile safety, emissions, or fuel economy legislation is specified as a function of the legislator's ideology, the economic interests of his constituents, and the more diffuse interests of the constituents.[2] The model identifies the key determinants

1. See Timothy F. Bresnahan and Dennis A. Yao, "The Nonpecuniary Costs of Automobile Emissions Standards," *Rand Journal of Economics,* vol. 16 (Winter 1985), pp. 437–55; and Sam Peltzman, "The Effects of Automobile Safety Regulation," *Journal of Political Economy,* vol. 83 (August 1975), pp. 677–725.

2. In the past decade legislative voting or roll call models have attracted significant attention from economists. See, for example, Sam Peltzman, "An Economic Interpretation of the History of Congressional Voting in the Twentieth Century," *American Economic Review,* vol. 75 (September 1985), pp. 656–75; Peltzman, "Constituent Interest and Congressional Voting," *Journal of Law and Economics,* vol. 27 (April 1984), pp. 181–210; Joseph P. Kalt and Mark A. Zupan, "Capture and Ideology in the Economic Theory of Politics," *American Economic Review,* vol. 74 (June 1984), pp. 279–300; and James B. Kau and Paul H. Rubin, "Self-Interest Ideology and Logrolling in Congressional Voting," *Journal of Law and Economics,* vol. 22 (October 1979), pp. 365–84.

of a legislator's votes and suggests a partial explanation for passage of the automobile regulations. We then illustrate how expectations of a regulation's effectiveness influence votes and how misperceptions of a regulation's effects can potentially explain the passage of socially undesirable automobile legislation.

Our analysis is admittedly based on a stylized characterization of legislative behavior and social welfare. We assume there is a direct link between legislators' votes and aggregate welfare, ignoring institutional considerations such as committees and logrolling.[3] We also do not consider the political role of legislation. For example, legislation to increase fuel economy may have been an effective threat to prod automakers to decrease vehicle weight and improve engine design at a time when consumer demand gave murky indications that such innovations would be rewarded in the market and when social benefits of fuel economy could not be appropriated by the automakers. Nevertheless, our study captures the key influences on legislators' voting behavior.

A Model of Legislative Voting

A voting or roll call model can capture the key determinants of a legislator's vote either on a particular piece of legislation or on a number of related bills. There are, however, serious obstacles to obtaining satisfactory results from an analysis of voting on a single bill or amendment. For any given vote, key variables may be unobserved or unmeasured. In addition, individual votes may be determined not by the particular issue but by extraneous considerations such as logrolling.[4] A more reliable approach is to aggregate votes on automobile legislation and construct a voting index.[5] Our index thus consists of votes by senators and representatives on legislation and amendments involving

3. In contrast to a compromise, in which two parties with different positions reach an agreement by modifying their respective positions, logrolling achieves agreement when parties simply agree to exchange support.

4. The econometric implication of this is that unobserved stochastic effects are likely to be correlated.

5. Following, for example, Kalt and Zupan the logit voting index is given by $I = \log [(r_i + 0.5)/(n_i - r_i + 0.5)]$, where n_i is the number of opportunities to vote on automobile regulations, and r_i is the number of times a vote was recorded in favor of regulation.

automobile safety, pollution, and fuel economy.[6] The votes that make up each index are presented in appendix A to this chapter.[7] They break down as two Senate and two House votes on automobile safety, ten Senate and eight House votes on automobile pollution regulation, and four Senate and five House votes on fuel economy, for a total of sixteen Senate votes and fifteen House votes. We include senators and representatives who voted on at least one of the regulatory issues, generating samples of 170 and 813 observations, respectively.[8]

Specification

The index is specified as a function of the economic interests of the legislator's constituents, diffuse constituency interests, and the legislator's ideology. The variables that control for constituent economic interests include state earnings from the motor vehicle and equipment industries as a fraction of total state earnings and the level of state membership in environmental organizations. Because the regulations adversely affect automobile-related earnings, at least in the short run,[9] we expect high levels of state earnings from the motor vehicle industry to have a negative effect on a legislator's likelihood of voting for the

6. For a summary of these regulations see Robert W. Crandall and others, *Regulating the Automobile* (Brookings, 1986), and appendix A to this chapter.

7. In constructing an index it is important that the votes be related. A factor analysis indicated that the votes within each regulatory category (safety, pollution, fuel economy) were highly related, but that votes in the pollution and fuel economy categories were not highly related to votes on safety. This suggests that the specification should contain some category-specific variables and even category dummy variables. Our specification contains category-specific variables. In addition, we estimated specifications that interacted category dummy variables with the ideology variable but did not obtain statistically different coefficients for ideology.

8. The votes are taken from *Congressional Quarterly Almanac*, various issues, 1966–77. Dummy variables are incorporated with explanatory variables so that legislators' votes are influenced only by variables that relate to the issues they voted on. Readers may be surprised at how few votes are studied. An exhaustive search of the *Congressional Quarterly Almanac* failed to turn up any more recorded votes, although there were many voice votes on these issues. Some recorded votes were discarded based on the factor analysis and a priori considerations (for example, votes that included issues not related to autos, such as energy, were, as expected, found to be unrelated to other votes).

9. Whether regulatory costs to producers will eventually be passed on to consumers depends on market structure.

automobile regulations, while high levels of constituent membership in environmental organizations would have a positive influence.[10]

Diffuse constituency interests reflect social as opposed to private economic concerns on matters such as pollution, automobile accidents, and fuel economy. Legislators respond to these interests by demonstrating leadership in coping with the issues involved.[11] We controlled for constituency interests that are affected by the automobile regulations by including pollutants from transportation sources, deaths and injuries from automobile accidents, and fuel performance in miles per gallon. We expected high pollution levels and increased numbers of accident victims to influence a legislator to vote for automobile regulations and high fuel performance to influence a legislator to vote against the regulations.

Ideology is typically measured by rating scales developed by groups such as the liberal Americans for Democratic Action and the conservative Americans for Constitutional Action. We used a combination of these scales to produce a variable that indicates the degree of liberal ideology. We expected increased liberalism to influence a legislator to vote for the automobile regulations. Notes to table 6-1 present precise definitions of variables and data sources.[12]

Generalized least squares estimates of the voting model for the House and Senate are presented in table 6-1.[13] The coefficients for both models were of the expected sign and of reasonable statistical reliability. The results give strong support for the constituency interest–ideology framework used here: legislators' votes on the automobile regulations are largely explained by different aspects of their constituents' interests and by their own ideological beliefs.[14] Because automobile regulations are

10. Initial estimations indicated that the effect of membership in environmental organizations was statistically insignificant; thus this variable is not included in our final results. The environmental organizations we considered are the same as those considered by Kalt and Zupan, "Capture and Ideology."

11. Time series behavior of variables that characterize automobile-related issues clearly attracted the attention of legislators (for example, the rising highway death rate in the early 1960s and the rapid rise in energy prices in the 1970s).

12. Initial specifications attempted to control for additional variables that might capture constituents' interests, such as the ratio of employment in the automobile industry to total employment, the price of gasoline, and contributions from political action committees. These effects, however, were found to be statistically insignificant.

13. Following Kalt and Zupan, "Capture and Ideology," the variance estimator for the logit voting index is given by $\text{Var}_i = [1/(r_i + 0.5)] + [1/(n_i - r_i + 0.5)]$.

14. A Chow test of whether coefficients for representatives and senators were

Table 6-1. Voting Model Estimation Results and Voting Index Elasticities

| Variable[b] | Estimation results[a] | | Elasticities | |
	House coefficient[c]	Senate coefficient[d]	House	Senate
Constant	−0.573	−0.572	. . .	. . .
	(0.071)	(0.157)		
Auto industry earnings[e]	−6.102	−7.513	−0.1053	−0.0870
	(0.993)	(2.500)		
Ideology[f]	0.020	0.022	1.0714	1.4278
	(0.001)	(0.002)		
Victims[g]	5.302	7.061	0.1437	0.1932
	(2.774)	(5.592)		
Pollution[h]	0.0015	0.0036	0.0748	0.1488
	(0.0007)	(0.0014)		
Miles per gallon[i]	−0.076	−0.067	−0.9852	−0.9519
	(0.006)	(0.010)		

Sources: Authors' calculations based on data from sources listed in table notes.
a. Standard errors are in parentheses.
b. All variables except ideology are constructed at the state level. Unfortunately, data were not available for representatives at the district level.
c. $R^2 = .31$; number of observations = 813.
d. $R^2 = .51$; number of observations = 170.
e. Earnings from the motor vehicle and equipment industry as a fraction of total state earnings. Data are from Department of Commerce, state survey data, 1958–84.
f. Based on scores from Americans for Democratic Action (ADA) and Americans for Constitutional Action (ACA) adjusted to exclude votes included in the dependent variable. Scores were determined by the equation [*ADA score* + (100 − *ACA score*)]/2. Data are from *Congressional Quarterly Weekly Report*, various years, 1966–77.
g. Deaths and injuries of auto accidents per licensed driver. Data are from Department of Health, Education, and Welfare, *Vital Statistics of the United States* (HEW, 1966, 1970, 1975); and Department of Transportation, Federal Highway Administration, *Fatal and Injury Accident Rates* (DOT, 1967, 1970, 1975).
h. Tons per year per area of carbon monoxide (CO), hydrocarbons (HC), and nitrogen oxides (NO_x) from transportation sources. Data are from Environmental Protection Agency, *National Air Monitoring Program: Air Quality and Emissions Trends Annual Report* (EPA, 1973).
i. Vehicle miles traveled (rural and urban) per gallon of fuel consumed. Data are from Automobile Manufacturers Association, *Highway Statistics, Automobile Facts and Figures* (AMA, various years).

primarily a form of social legislation, it is not surprising that ideology has some influence on votes by members of Congress.[15]

The voting index elasticities presented in table 6-1 indicate that representatives' and senators' votes respond similarly to changes in variables that characterize their constituents' interests but that senators' votes are more responsive than representatives' to changes in ideology.[16]

statistically different could not be carried out because we did not have House and Senate votes on the same legislation.
15. Attempts were made to analyze the effect of ideology by using the residualization procedure in Kalt and Zupan, "Capture and Ideology," and by controlling for other variables such as political party. However, this did not significantly alter the results reported here.
16. The voting index elasticity with respect to a given variable can be interpreted as the percentage change in the probability of voting for automobile regulations that results from a 1 percent change in the given variable.

This finding is reasonable because senators' longer terms of office and broader constituencies give them greater latitude for independence in policymaking.[17]

One aspect of the results, however, is puzzling. If legislators' votes on automobile regulations were significantly influenced by their constituents' interests, why has Congress passed legislation that is widely believed, based on retrospective studies, to be at variance with these interests? We address this question in the next section by considering legislators' expectations of the effectiveness of automobile regulations.

Expectations and Voting

The votes of members of Congress are based partly on their expectations as to whether the legislation's goals will be met. If the actual effects of a regulation are substantially different from its expected effects, then socially undesirable legislation could have been passed despite legislators' having the best interests of their constituencies in mind. Table 6-2 shows estimates of the expected and actual effects of the automobile regulations on automakers' earnings, number of accident victims, automobile pollution, and fuel efficiency. Although the estimates of legislators' expectations should be taken only as suggestive, it is nonetheless striking that the actual effectiveness of the automobile regulations (under optimistic *and* pessimistic scenarios) is considerably less than their expected effectiveness. Automobile safety, air pollution, and fuel efficiency were not improved as much as expected, while the costs of the regulations were higher than expected.

The figures in table 6-2 suggest that one of the reasons most of the legislation passed was that members of Congress did not have good forecasts of the likely effects of the legislation. If they had known the legislation would be so costly and so relatively ineffective, they might have taken a different approach or altered it.[18]

A model that could capture the effects of those expectations would allow simulations to be conducted to see if changes in expectations

17. This issue is discussed further in Kalt and Zupan, "Capture and Ideology."

18. One might argue that the political cost of legislators' incorrect forecasts is reduced if constituents make similar forecast errors. It would be erroneous, however, to claim that bad judgment, even if shared by others, will never come back to haunt a legislator.

Table 6-2. Estimates of Expected and Actual Changes in Automaker Earnings, Number
of Accident Victims, Pollution, and Fuel Performance from Automobile Regulations

Variable	Expected changes	Actual changes[a] Pessimistic estimate	Optimistic estimate
Earnings[b]	0–5 percent decrease	15 percent decrease	7 percent decrease
Victims[c]	30–50 percent decrease	no change	20–30 percent decrease
Pollution[d]	90 percent decrease	10 percent decrease	40 percent decrease
Miles per gallon[e]	75 percent increase	no change	no change

Sources: Authors' calculations based on data described in table notes.

a. Robert W. Crandall and others, *Regulating the Automobile* (Brookings, 1986). These estimates identify the effect of the regulations on earnings, victims, pollution, and fuel economy, holding other influences constant. Thus if fuel economy increased after the fuel economy regulations were in effect but this increase was caused by factors other than regulation, then the estimated actual change in fuel economy due to regulation is zero.

b. In a stock market event study the authors found that the market's expectations regarding U.S. automobile firms' earnings were basically unaffected by any of the automobile regulations. See Dennis Sheehan and Clifford Winston, "Regulating the Automobile Industry: Economic Effects and Theories of Regulation" (unpublished paper, Brookings, August 1984).

c. Testimony before Congress on the National Traffic and Motor Vehicle Safety Act of 1966 indicates that certain mandated safety features on automobiles were widely expected to reduce significantly the escalating incidence of auto fatalities. Joseph Kelner, president of the American Trial Lawyers Association, testified that his group believed auto fatalities would be reduced by 50 percent if safety features were mandatory in new automobiles. See *Congressional Quarterly Almanac 1966* (Washington, D.C.: Congressional Quarterly Service, 1967), p. 276.

d. The Clean Air Act of 1970 included a provision that required 1975 model year cars to emit 90 percent less hydrocarbon and carbon monoxide pollution than 1970 model year cars and 1976 model year cars to emit 90 percent less nitrogen oxide pollution than 1971 model year cars. The bill was thus expected eventually to reduce pollution from automobile sources by 90 percent as post-1975 model year autos were purchased and pre-1975 unregulated autos were scrapped. See *Congressional Quarterly Almanac 1970* (Washington, D.C.: Congressional Quarterly Service, 1967), p. 472.

e. A provision of the Energy Conservation and Oil Policy Act of 1975 required that the average fuel economy for passenger cars be at least 27.5 miles per gallon in 1985. This figure represents a 75 percent increase in fuel economy from the 1975 average of 15.79 miles per gallon. Thus legislators expected to see a 75 percent improvement in fuel economy as 1985 model year cars replaced the earlier models. See *Congressional Quarterly Almanac 1975* (Washington, D.C.: Congressional Quarterly Service, 1976), p. 223.

would alter the predicted voting outcome. Thus we respecify the explanatory variables, with the exception of ideology, as expected changes. For example, the victims variable is specified as Δ *victims* = *expected victims* − *victims*, where *expected victims* is derived from the expected changes in table 6-2 and *victims* is the variable used previously.[19] This respecification will simply rescale each of the coefficients in the levels model in rough proportion to how each explanatory variable is adjusted; t statistics will be unchanged, and the signs will adjust in accordance with the expected change. For example, the sign of Δ *victims* will now be positive because the greater the expected change (decrease) in *victims*, the higher the likelihood that a legislator will support legislation.

When the expectations model is estimated with actual values of the

19. Formally, the new specification is given by

$$\text{Index} = \beta_0 + \beta_1 \text{ideology} + \beta_2 \Delta \text{earnings} + \beta_3 \Delta \text{victims} + \beta_4 \Delta \text{pollution} + \beta_5 \Delta \text{mpg},$$

where for a given variable X_i, $\Delta X_i = E(X_i) - X_i$.

Table 6-3. Prediction of Index Based on Substituting Actual Changes for Expected Changes[a]

Actual changes	House predicted index	Senate predicted index
Earnings decrease 7 percent; victims decrease 20 percent	−.155	.088
Earnings decrease 15 percent; pollution decreases 10 percent	−.319	.004
Earnings decrease 15 percent; victims—no change; pollution decreases 10 percent	−.426	−.102

Source: Authors' calculations.
a. Predicted index is calculated by substituting the actual changes noted above for the expected changes and holding other variables at their expected change.

regulatory-affected variables (based on table 6-2) substituted for the expected values and the voting index based on actual changes predicted, the findings of congressional support for automobile legislation change significantly. An index value greater than zero indicates that support for the legislation exceeds 50 percent, on average, and that the legislation, on average, would pass by majority vote.[20] Based on actual votes on the automobile legislation, the mean value of the Senate voting index is 0.229 and the mean value of the House index is −0.040.[21] Table 6-3 presents some illustrative predictions of the voting index based on substituting the actual results of the safety, emissions, and fuel economy regulations for the changes expected by the legislators when they approved the legislation. If senators had had perfect foresight, then for at least one pessimistic actual scenario, the automobile regulations, on average, would not have been supported (that is, the predicted index is negative). For the House the likelihood of legislative passage would also have been significantly lowered, on average, if representatives had had perfect foresight. Although this exercise is intended to be illustrative rather than a rigorous analysis of what the voting indexes would be if legislators had perfect foresight, it does suggest that the passage of what have turned out to be largely undesirable automobile regulations (based on retrospective studies) can be partly attributed to congressional misperceptions of the legislation's effects.[22]

20. This does not imply, of course, that any individual regulation, including the most important ones, would necessarily pass by a majority vote.

21. The mean value of the House index is negative because a number of amendments were rejected by large margins (see appendix A to this chapter).

22. Michael E. Levine argues that airline regulation was imposed by a Congress

Conclusions

The past few decades have witnessed a number of crises in automobile-related issues, including safety, fuel economy, pollution, U.S. industry profitability, and employment. Public policies to address these issues have often been formulated and implemented in an atmosphere of crisis. Retrospective analyses of these policies have often concluded that they were not in the public interest, but have left open the question of why they were supported by a political body presumably concerned with its constituents' interests. A possible answer is that analysis of these policies was based on flawed information and that misperceptions of the policies' effects were responsible for their legislative support.[23]

Why doesn't the threat of election defeat make legislators take more care in their policy formulations so that grievous misperceptions do not occur? Why aren't policies quickly reversed when they are determined to be ineffective? In the case of automobile policies, a partial answer to the first question is that in the crisis atmosphere in which these policies were formulated, long-run effectiveness could be ignored because most constituents were unlikely to care about or even be cognizant of the actual effects of an automobile policy by the time its effects were clearly determined. This suggests, as an answer to the second question, that undesirable policies will be reversed when the cost of information about their effectiveness is low (that is, it is widely believed they are ineffective or at least it is easy to provide convincing evidence that they are ineffective) and when they are sufficiently visible (for example, because of another crisis) to generate benefits to political entrepreneurs who question their desirability.

The failure of the political process to generate sound evaluations of proposed automobile public policies raises the issue of whether the effects of the policies were inherently unpredictable or whether the

that, while attempting to act in the public interest, made a mistake. See "Revisionism Revised? Airline Deregulation and the Public Interest," *Law and Contemporary Problems*, vol. 44 (Winter 1981), pp. 179–95.

23. The one policy that we found to be socially beneficial, the 55 mph speed limit, was justified largely because of its unanticipated contribution to reducing automobile deaths and injuries.

Crisis circumstances may lead members of Congress to pass legislation simply to avoid blame, which can in turn lead (in retrospect) to ineffective policies. Our analysis indicates, however, that legislators expected the automobile legislation to be effective.

effects could have been foreseen if an appropriate framework and methodology for evaluation had been developed. If the effects were unpredictable, then it would have been advisable for legislators to include some sunset provisions in the legislation. If the likely effects could be determined in advance, then there was scope for review agencies to determine the desirability of the legislation before it was implemented.

The primary effects of recent automobile public policies—particularly the socially undesirable ones—could have been determined by a sound economic framework and careful analysis. The social cost of these policies demands that such analyses be undertaken in response to policies proposed in the future.

Appendix A: Votes Included in Senators' and Representatives' Voting Index

Senate

The following amendments and pieces of legislation were included in the senators' index. Several amendments and pieces of legislation were not included because voice votes only were recorded. Fourteen amendments and six pieces of legislation were recorded only as voice votes.

Safety

S.3005.   National Traffic and Motor Vehicle Safety Act, requiring the secretary of commerce to establish federal safety performance standards for motor vehicles and tires, conduct federal safety research activities, and expand a national driver register service. Passed 76–0, June 24, 1966.

S.3005.   National Traffic and Motor Vehicle Safety Act amendment to eliminate the requirement that patents, information, uses, and processes developed in safety research with more than "minimal" federal aid be freely and fully available to the general public. Rejected 35–43, June 24, 1966.

Emission control

S.2772.   Clean Air Standards to postpone the effective date of the

1976 model year auto emission standards for hydrocarbons and carbon monoxide until the 1977 model year. Passed 85–0, December 17, 1973.

S.2772. Clean Air Standards amendment to postpone until the 1978 model year the effective date of interim 1975 and statutory 1976 model year auto emission standards for hydrocarbons and carbon monoxide. Rejected 19–67, December 17, 1973.

S.3219. Clean Air Act amendments to revise air pollution cleanup requirements and schedules for automobiles and stationary pollution sources. Passed 78–13, August 5, 1976.

S.3219. Clean Air Act amendment to require auto manufacturers to comply with all statutory emission standards in 1979 instead of 1980. Rejected 30–61, August 5, 1976

S.3219. Clean Air Act amendment to require the statutory 0.4 grams per mile standard for nitrogen oxides instead of relaxing it to 1.0 grams per mile. Rejected 33–58, August 5, 1976.

S.252. Clean Air Act amendment to delete provisions requiring that the nitrogen oxide standard for automobile emissions be reduced to 0.4 gram per mile by model year 1983, leaving provisions to require a study by the Environmental Protection Agency into the health impact, cost, and technological feasibility of the 0.4 nitrogen oxide standard. Passed 51–43, June 8, 1977.

S.252. Clean Air Act amendments: motion to table, and thus kill, part 1 of the Griffin amendment to specify that the delay in meeting standards provided for small companies would apply only to U.S. manufacturers. Passed 56–38, June 9, 1977.

S.252. Clean Air Act amendments: motion to table, and thus kill, part 2 of the Griffin amendment to allow a one-year extension of whatever emission deadlines the Senate approved for small manufacturers. Passed 60–35, June 9, 1977.

S.252. Clean Air Act amendment to establish a delayed interim compliance schedule for any manufacturer of less than 300,000 cars a year that does not manufacture its own pollution equipment. Passed 77–16, June 9, 1977.

S.252. Clean Air Act amendment to maintain existing emission standards for hydrocarbons and carbon monoxide for two years, until 1980; require 10 percent of 1979 cars to meet a one-gram nitrogen oxide standard; and make one gram the general nitrogen oxide standard by 1989, but allow waivers to encourage production of innovative engine and emission systems. Passed 56–38, June 9, 1977.

Fuel economy

S.1883.   Mandatory auto fuel economy standards bill to direct the secretary of transportation to establish and enforce mandatory fuel economy performance standards for new cars and light duty trucks in model years 1977–85 and establish a research and development program aimed at creating a prototype car with high fuel efficiency that meets pollution and safety requirements. Passed 63–21, July 15, 1975.

S.1883.   Mandatory auto fuel economy standards amendment to make the mandatory fuel economy standards apply to 1978 model year vehicles instead of beginning with 1977 model year vehicles. Rejected 27–57, July 15, 1975.

S.2057.   Energy conservation: motion to table, and thus kill, the Riegle amendment to delete from the bill language that would ban production of automobiles not meeting standards of fuel efficiency specified in the bill. Passed 52–27, September 12, 1977.

S.2057.   Energy conservation: motion to table, and thus kill, the Riegle amendment to invalidate language in the bill banning production of fuel-inefficient automobiles if the legislation as enacted included a tax on the purchase of such vehicles. Passed 52–28, September 12, 1977.

House

The following amendments and pieces of legislation were included in the representatives' index. There were twenty-one amendments and five pieces of legislation that were recorded only as voice votes.

Safety

S.3005.   National Traffic and Motor Vehicle Safety Act: conference report on the bill requiring the secretary of commerce to establish federal safety performance standards for motor vehicles and tires, conduct federal safety research activities, and expand a national driver register service. Adopted 365–0, August 31, 1966.

H.R.11627.   Motor vehicle repair costs to require federal standards for front and rear bumpers to minimize damage to automobiles in low-speed collisions and establish a consumer information program to study and make available to the public comparative costs of vehicle repairs. Passed 254–38, May 22, 1972.

Emission control

H.R.11450.   National Energy Emergency Act to extend through the 1977 model year the interim federal vehicle emission standards for the 1975 model year. Passed 199–180, December 15, 1973.

H.R. 11450.   National Energy Emergency Act amendment to suspend auto emission standards through January 1, 1977, or the date on which the president declares that the petroleum shortage is at an end, whichever is later, in all areas except specified regions with significantly high pollution levels. Rejected 180–210, December 14, 1973.

H.R.11450.   National Energy Emergency Act amendment to suspend auto emission standards through January 1, 1976, or the date on which the president declares that petroleum shortages are over, whichever is later, in all areas except specified regions with significantly high pollution levels. Rejected 170–205, December 14, 1973.

H.R.14368.   Energy supply and coordination amendment to suspend auto emission controls in the United States until 1977 except for those areas designated as having heavy pollution levels. Rejected 169–221, May 1, 1974.

H.R.10498.   Clean Air Act amendment to require final auto emission standards to take effect in 1981 and tighter interim standards in 1978–80. Rejected 75–313, September 15, 1976.

H.R. 10498.   Clean Air Act amendment to postpone final auto emission standards until 1982 and allow the Environmental Protection Agency to modify the final standard for nitrogen oxide. Passed 224–169, September 15, 1976.

H.R. 10498.   Clean Air Act amendment to delay automobile emission schedules by one additional year and waive certain restrictions on small diesel engines. Rejected 190–202, May 26, 1977.

H.R. 6161.   Clean Air Act amendment to delay and relax automobile emission standards, reduce the warranties for emission control devices, and make other changes in existing law regarding mobile sources of air pollution. Passed 255–139, May 26, 1977.

Fuel economy

H.R. 6860.   Energy taxes amendment to impose a tax on each inefficient car providing fuel mileage below certain standards as well as a tax on each manufacturer or importer whose cars provide average efficiency below certain standards. Rejected 166–235, June 12, 1975.

H.R. 6860.   Energy taxes amendment to prohibit any automobile manufacturer to build cars providing fuel mileage below certain standards starting in 1982. Rejected 79–319, June 12, 1975.

H.R. 6860.   Energy taxes amendment to impose a fine on the manufacturer of any car that provides fuel mileage below certain standards. Rejected 128–271, June 12, 1975.

H.R. 6860.   Energy taxes amendment to impose fines on automobile manufacturers or importers if the average fuel efficiency provided by all their cars falls below certain standards. The fines, effective for 1978, 1979, and 1980 model years, would be $5.00 for each one-tenth of a mile per gallon by which the average standard was missed multiplied by the number of cars built or imported. Passed 306–86, June 12, 1975.

H.R. 7014.   Energy Conservation and Oil Policy Act amendment to delete from the bill the 1985 goal for auto efficiency of a fleetwide average of twenty-eight miles a gallon for American automobile producers. Rejected 117–284, September 17, 1975.

CHAPTER SEVEN

Public Policy and Auto Industry Evolution

CLIFFORD WINSTON

THE RESULTS of this study suggest that for the foreseeable future U.S. automakers will compete relatively successfully with foreign manufacturers for a substantial share of the U.S. market. This development is particularly likely if the government abandons trade restrictions on Japanese autos and macroeconomic policy succeeds in keeping the dollar at a ratio to the yen that preserves competitiveness. American consumers will thus benefit from a highly competitive automobile industry in an unrestricted market, and U.S. automakers will experience adequate profits. U.S. employment in the auto industry will, however, be reduced because manufacturers will continue with outsourcing and other cost-cutting measures.

Because the American automobile market is the world's most lucrative, all automakers recognize the importance of competing in it effectively. The U.S. market continues to attract new entrants trying to find niches and thus generates new responses by established companies. Korean and Yugoslavian automakers have recently challenged Japanese and American companies in the low-cost, small-car market. Japanese automakers are moving up to challenge American companies in the mid-sized car market. Manufacturers of high-priced, high-performance vehicles such as Jaguar and BMW are anticipating new challenges to their market position by offering factory-guaranteed used cars.

American companies are entering into alliances with foreign manufacturers to compete more effectively at both the high and low ends of the market and to solidify their established advantage in producing mid-

103

sized autos. Ford and General Motors have lined up foreign sources to help produce low-cost small cars. In addition, General Motors is offering a low-priced version of the Chevette for 1987 and Chrysler a low-priced version of the Dodge Omni/Plymouth Horizon. In the high-priced, high-performance market, Cadillac is introducing the Allante manufactured by an Italian design and coachwork company, Chrysler plans to offer a vehicle produced by Maserati, and the Merkur, Ford's entry, is manufactured in Germany. Finally, American joint ventures with Japanese companies will produce cars in the middle of the spectrum. General Motors and Toyota are already producing cars, Chrysler is planning to undertake a joint venture with Mitsubishi, and Ford has planned a marketing arrangement with Mazda. Besides these alliances, several Japanese companies as well as Volvo and Volkswagen have established or plan to establish production capacity in the United States.

Despite the anticipated changes in competition, production strategies have converged. American and foreign companies are building cars with components from throughout the world. American companies are using parts manufactured in Brazil, Mexico, and Korea; Japanese companies are importing parts from Korea; Volkswagen plans to import a Brazilian-made vehicle; and so on. In addition, U.S. companies are building some specialized cars with smaller markets at production runs that are low by American standards but comparable to standards of foreign firms.

The corporate alliances and similarities in production strategies and manufacturing locations will undoubtedly blur the distinction between American and foreign vehicles. This should be, however, of little concern to American automakers and consumers. U.S. automakers seem well positioned to compete effectively and, at appropriate exchange rates, are capable of keeping their production costs competitive. The American companies have largely adjusted to an industry that has become increasingly internationalized, an adjustment that should ensure adequate profits as global automobile competition evolves. American consumers should benefit from the increased competition, which should hold down prices and increase vehicle quality and variety. Anticipated automobile innovations may even make safety a key selling point.

The evolution of the industry will, however, exacerbate the reductions in automobile employment. Increased outsourcing by U.S. companies will hurt employment, and outsourcing by foreign companies that establish U.S. production facilities will modify any employment gains they might otherwise create.[1] At the same time, U.S. companies are also trying to trim executive and clerical employment to cut costs.

Government can effectively aid American automakers through macroeconomic policy leading to exchange rates that ensure cost competitiveness and to a growth rate that generates adequate demand. The companies do not need trade restrictions. Indeed, given the increased internationalization of automobile production, trade restrictions would seriously hinder the automakers' evolution. The increased level of competition in the American market should not only satisfy consumers' need for quality and variety but satisfy social goals such as fuel economy and safety. It is highly unlikely that regulations will be needed to achieve these goals.

We have recommended public policy that supports the continued evolution of the industry, an evolution that will reduce automobile employment. Although labor has traditionally supported trade protection to preserve automobile jobs, such protection would be especially inappropriate in the evolving competitive environment. Anticipated employment reductions are not attributable to import penetration per se, but to the automakers' adjustment to an industry that has become highly internationalized. Almost all major automakers recognize the need to make use of the low-cost labor available in other countries and acknowledge the importance of having lean executive staffs to maintain cost competitiveness.

To be sure, political pressures will demand that some action be taken to aid workers from industries that are significantly reducing their work force in response to increased internationalization. Employment adjustment assistance is a better alternative than trade restrictions. This assistance will partially compensate those whose welfare will be hurt by the adjustments American automakers must make to be a leading force in world automobile production.

1. The Automotive Parts and Accessories Association estimates that 60 percent of the parts in an American-assembled Japanese car are imported.

Index